BREXIT UNMASKED

To all at Suffolk University
With best wishes.
Albert Kemp

A. E. Kemp

First published 2023

Copyright © Albert Kemp 2023

The right of Albert Kemp to be identified as the author of this work has been asserted in accordance with the Copyright, Designs & Patents Act 1988.

All rights reserved. No part of this book may be reproduced, stored in a retrieval system, or transmitted in any form or by any means, electronic, electrostatic, magnetic tape, mechanical, photocopying, recording or otherwise, without the written permission of the copyright holder.

Published under licence by Brown Dog Books and
The Self-Publishing Partnership Ltd, 10b Greenway Farm, Bath Rd,
Wick, nr. Bath BS30 5RL

www.selfpublishingpartnership.co.uk

ISBN printed book: 978-1-83952-595-7
ISBN e-book: 978-1-83952-596-4

Cover design by Kevin Rylands
Internal design by Andrew Easton

Printed and bound in the UK

This book is printed on FSC® certified paper

BREXIT UNMASKED

The memoirs and opinions
of a nonagenarian

ALBERT KEMP

Contents

Chapter 1	A Wonderful Opportunity Spurned	6
Chapter 2	My Immediate Family	13
Chapter 3	My Early Life and Parental Influences	31
Chapter 4	The Gathering Storm	50
Chapter 5	The 2016 Referendum	56
Chapter 6	The Aftermath and the 2019 General Election	66
Chapter 7	Brexit and the Economy	76
Chapter 8	Brexit and Immigration	84
Chapter 9	Freedom and Sovereignty	90
Chapter 10	Covid-19 and Brexit	95
Chapter 11	The Way Ahead	102
Endnotes		113

Chapter 1

A Wonderful Opportunity Spurned

It was early September 1956 and I was travelling on a train which I had joined at a channel port in northern France. My intention was to change trains in Paris, and then proceed eastwards to Strasbourg, where I had arranged to have a two-week stay. I was twenty-eight years of age (approaching twenty-nine), and my purpose in going to Strasbourg was to take a two-week study course in the French language at Strasbourg University. During the 1950s, I made several such trips to universities in France for the same purpose. As a junior civil servant, I did not have a great deal of money to throw around, and, as the food and accommodation were heavily subsidised by the French government, these vacation courses were very attractive to me. They gave me an opportunity to go to interesting places, meet up with interesting people of about my own age and, hopefully, improve my French at the same time. My choice of Strasbourg in 1956 was made purely at random from a brochure that the French authorities produced annually. Little did I realise that this choice of location would influence my thinking about European co-operation for the rest of my life.

On the way to Paris, I treated myself to an excellent, if expensive, meal on the train, and had some congenial company in the form of two young

UNIVERSITÉ DE STRASBOURG

FACULTÉ DES LETTRES

Certificat d'Assiduité

Le Directeur soussigné des **Cours de Vacances** atteste par la présente

que Monsieur Albert Edward KEMP

né le 30.10.1927 à Londres

de nationalité britannique habitant Londres

a suivi assidûment les Cours de français

organisés par la Faculté, du 10 septembre au 22 septembre 1956

Strasbourg, le 22 septembre 1956

A copy of the certificate that I received from Strasbourg University in September, 1956. It is in a format that was normally used by French Universities at that period, when certificates were provided to students at the completion of a vacation course.

American males who were seated at my table. I enjoyed chatting with them, and exchanging views about various topics. They appeared to be in their early twenties and were, if I remember correctly, travelling to Lyons. I had the impression that they might be Mormons – I knew that the Church of the Latter-Day Saints frequently sent their younger brethren abroad to do evangelical work – but did not attempt to confirm this idea. On my arrival at the Gare du Nord, I proceeded towards the Gare de l'Est by way of the Paris Metro. A rather amusing incident took place in the Metro when a large Austrian gentleman, who was struggling with two suitcases, approached me and asked if I could help him find the train that he needed. Of all the people who were in the Metro at that point in time, I was probably the least qualified to give directions to anybody. However, I manfully took him under my wing, and managed to put him onto an underground train that I hoped would take him to his required main-line station. I then made my own way to the Gare de l'Est, where I embarked on a train to Strasbourg.

The journey to Strasbourg was, as far as I can recall, uneventful, and upon my arrival I made my way immediately to the university. The latter was a large, dour-looking but imposing, structure, which I gathered had been built during the latter part of the nineteenth century when Germany was in control of the Alsace. After signing in, I was shown to my sleeping quarters, and to the university restaurant which was known as 'Fec'! With the passing of so many years, I cannot remember whether these facilities were in the main building or a separate annexe. However, I slept in a dormitory which was normally used by the full-time students, and the food provided by Fec was excellent! Over the next day or two I quickly made the acquaintance of many of the other vacation students who were present. They were predominantly male (although there were a sprinkling of female students) and most of them appeared to be Belgian or Dutch. There were also people from the Scandinavian countries and a few Poles. I do not recall encountering any German students (although it seems likely that there must have been some) and I thought that they were possibly still unsure about the kind of reception that they might get. A small number of British students (mainly young people who were doing full-time studies at British universities) were also present.

Outside of the curriculum that we followed, I soon found that the main topic of conversation was the establishment of the European Economic Community (EEC), which was due to be formally brought into being in March 1957. Although I was well aware that this important event was going to take place in about six months' time, there had, to the best of my knowledge, been very little publicity about it in the UK, and what had been written had seemed to me to be fairly negative. The fact that the UK had decided not to join the EEC as a founder member was clearly a huge disappointment to many of my fellow students (particularly the Belgian and Dutch people), and the extent to which they deplored the UK's absence was a revelation to me. It was evident that they had wanted the UK to play a leading role in the project; hence their disappointment that this was not to be the case. Many of the students appeared to be of about my age or somewhat older, and their enthusiasm for European co-operation seemed, in part, to stem from their wartime experiences. Although over eleven years had elapsed since the end of the Second World War, their memories of what life had been like under enemy occupation were still raw and they were determined to ensure that nothing like it should ever happen again in their lifetimes. I can recall a Belgian student saying to me in English on one occasion, "We should forgive but not forget". One of the voluntary evening lectures that I attended consisted of a lengthy dissertation about the objectives and aspirations of the EEC, and although I could not understand all that the French professor was saying, I was able to get the gist of it. Most of his information suggested strongly to me that the UK would lose out badly by not being a founder-member.

Albert Kemp

My time in Strasbourg was not devoted entirely to serious matters. I liked the city very much and spent a good part of the daylight hours wandering around its ancient thoroughfares. I had known from previous experiences that the unattached young women in most places usually went around in pairs, and that, if one wished to make their acquaintance, it was advisable to team up with somebody. I was fortunate enough to encounter a twenty-four-year-old Norwegian who was also travelling solo. He was a full-time student of foreign languages and we did a lot of sightseeing together. His English was impeccable, and I was not surprised to learn that he had lived for two years in the west London district of Hammersmith. One of the places that we went to was the Council of Europe. Another was the famous old cathedral; a lovely old Gothic building which, as was usually the case with medieval cathedrals, had taken well over one hundred years to construct. Although magnificent, the building had a slightly lopsided appearance; an impression derived from the fact that it had only one spire rather than the two originally planned. During our visit we were able to make our way to the top of the cathedral, from which point we had a superb view of the city. In the evenings we usually visited the local hostelries (preferably the ones where music and dancing were available), of which there were a good number. Towards the end of our time in Strasbourg, my Norwegian friend gave me his card on which he was described as a philologist, and expressed the hope that we might meet again sometime. I regret to say that I cannot bring his name to mind, although I can still visualise him quite well. Our paths never crossed again, but I will always remember him as a very likeable fellow and good companion.

Before I left Strasbourg, I had become convinced that the UK was making a huge mistake in remaining aloof from the EEC. The advantages that would accrue from being a founder member seemed to be overwhelming, and I found it difficult to believe that the UK government had given the matter serious consideration. I felt confident that the new coalition of European countries would, in time, prove to be a huge success, and that it would be of considerable benefit to their economies and, just as importantly, to their relationships with one another. A prominent role in the new European alliance would, I considered, give the UK a far more realistic and effective standing in the world than the great-power position that it was attempting to project. Upon my return to London, I wondered whether there was any way in which the government could be persuaded to revisit the possibility of being a founder-member of the EEC before it was too late. I soon realised, however, that there was very little that I, a complete nobody, could do. I had no political affiliations, and the Labour opposition of the day seemed, if anything, even more parochial than the Anthony Eden government. Moreover, headlines in the press had for several months been dominated by Nasser's nationalisation of the Suez Canal. Fears had subsequently been expressed in the media that Egypt would be unable to operate the Suez Canal efficiently, and that Egypt and other African countries would migrate into the Soviet orbit. All this had seemed very exaggerated, as I thought that the Egyptians would soon show themselves more than capable of running the waterway, and I doubted that they would want to get rid of one colonial master in order to adopt another. I did pen a quick letter to a newspaper. I believe that it was The Times, although it might possibly have been The Telegraph. In it, I said that I was concerned that the UK was losing a great opportunity in opting not to become a founder-member of the EEC, and asked whether they could do anything to persuade the government to take a fresh look at the matter. I received no reply from the newspaper, and I presumed that my letter had disappeared straight into their wastepaper basket.

A little over a month later, my fears that the UK government was fully preoccupied with Egypt were confirmed when Britain, France and Israel launched a pre-arranged invasion of Egypt. Although the invasion enjoyed brief military successes, it was, in political terms, a total disaster. It invoked worldwide condemnation in the United Nations, and, faced with threats by the UK's main ally, the USA, of economic sanctions if the UK did not immediately stop the invasion and withdraw its forces, the UK was forced into a humiliating climbdown. When the UK ceased its operations and began to withdraw its forces from Egypt, the other invading powers, France and Israel, had little choice but to do likewise. Israel had, in fact, been able to obtain some benefits from the operation, but both the UK and France had been unable to realise any of their main objectives. One of these was to topple Nasser, but the ill-judged venture served only to greatly increase his prestige, particularly in the Arab world. The entire Suez fiasco had also attracted considerable criticism within the UK, and hardly anyone I knew was prepared to believe the story that Anthony Eden had concocted. If all this did not lead the UK to reappraise its true position in the world, then what could, I speculated. When Harold Macmillan took over the premiership following Anthony Eden's resignation in January 1957, I wondered whether he might be the leader who could persuade his colleagues in Parliament and the general public that the UK's future lay with Europe. It soon became apparent, however, that his immediate concern was, not surprisingly, to repair the UK's relations with the USA. By 1961, Harold Macmillan had decided that the UK would be better off if it entered the EEC, but by then it was far too late. General de Gaulle had returned to power in France in June 1958, and he was implacably opposed to the UK's membership. Whilst the Suez debacle in 1956 is nowadays regarded, rightly, as a watershed in Britain's relations with the world and of great importance, our country's failure in the same year to opt for EEC founder-membership is generally overlooked or ignored. This is a pity, as both episodes were, in their different ways, of equal importance to the UK's future development and prosperity.

Chapter 2

My Immediate Family

In order to explain more fully the influences that helped to inform my beliefs and opinions, I think that I should write a little about my family and myself. In an attempt to do this, I have searched hard and long into my memories for people outside of my immediate family who might have guided me during my childhood, without success. I would love, for example, to be able to point to a particular schoolteacher who was instrumental in inspiring my beliefs and attitudes. The truth is, however, that my formal education was so disrupted and intermittent, and punctuated by long enforced absences, that I rarely had a teacher for more than one term. It rapidly became clear, therefore, that the main influences in my early life were my parents. This should not have been a surprise, as all three of my immediate family were, in their different ways, remarkable people. Another reason why I have decided to provide personal information about my family and myself is that in discussions with other people about Brexit both during the 2016 referendum campaign and more recently, my support of Remain has occasionally been described as unpatriotic. I hope that this chapter and the following one will demonstrate that, whatever we may have lacked as a family, it was not a lack of patriotism.

Albert Kemp

These photographs show my parents and brother. The upper photographs show my mother and father in about 1915 (possibly a year or two later in the case of my mother). The lower photographs show my brother and my father, and were taken in 1940.

I was born in October 1927 in the east London borough of Shoreditch into a small, but politically aware, family. My father and mother (both Eastenders who had been born and had grown up close to my own birthplace) were extremely kind and loving parents, and, as I realised in later years, remarkably tolerant and helpful towards their somewhat peculiar second son! I had only one sibling; a brother who was a little over seven years older than I. Although I admired him a great deal and remained on good terms with him throughout his life, we were never close – the age gap was too great. Moreover, we were temperamentally very different. My brother, Henry Arthur Kemp junior (known as Harry), was a much more mercurial character, and had a local reputation as something of a daredevil. I, on the other hand, was far more placid and studious by nature. When Harry was about fifteen and on a training exercise with sea cadets, it was reported that he had been the first to jump off the upper deck of an old wooden battleship (the cadets' accommodation) into the sea. He had been, from a very early age, a strong swimmer –an ability that, as I will recount in due course, probably saved his life seven years later.

Both of my parents were extremely important to my early development, but in discussing them I would like, for no particular reason, to start first with my father. Henry Arthur Kemp senior was born in September 1894, just a few hundred yards away from my place of birth thirty-three years later. At the time of his birth, he had two older brothers, Jack and Frank, who would have been aged, respectively, about two and four years. Later, the family was completed by the arrival of three younger sisters, Florence, Beatrice and Ivy, the eldest of whom, Florence, was around two years younger than my father. The head of the household, William Francis Kemp (known generally as Francis) and his wife, Elizabeth, although far from affluent, appear to have been reasonably comfortably off. Like his ancestors for several generations, Francis had trained as a master cabinet maker and had a small woodworking business. He had at least one assistant who was apprenticed to him, and from the certificates that I hold it seems that he specialised in making tables. Unfortunately, the family's comfortable life together came to an abrupt end in the spring of 1908 when, after becoming completely soaked, my grandfather developed pneumonia and died within twenty-four hours. The narrative, as relayed to me by my father, was that Francis had attended some kind of celebration with workmates, had had too much to drink and had decided to take a swim in the local canal. It was mid-April, and one can only imagine what the temperature of the water must have been like. Present at my grandfather's death at the age of forty-eight was, according to his death certificate, one Frederick McDaniel (said to be a nephew). This relationship was probably correct, as it seems likely that Frederick McDaniel was his apprentice and, in those days, such assistants were frequently drawn from younger family members.

As can easily be imagined, my grandfather's premature death represented a total disaster for the family. He had been the family's only real breadwinner, and in early 1908 there were no safety nets. The eldest of the three brothers, my uncle Frank who was about eighteen, had decided against becoming a woodworker and had joined the army about two years earlier as a boy soldier. Although I am not certain about this, I believe that he was in India at the time of his father's death. The second son (my uncle Jack), who was about fifteen at this time, was undergoing an apprenticeship in the family trade with an uncle. With a mother and three younger sisters to be supported, it must have been obvious that any reserves that they might have had would soon be depleted and that it would be a desperate fight to keep the family out of the workhouse. My father, a thirteen-year-old schoolboy, had no choice, therefore, but to leave school immediately and seek any form of employment that he might be able to get. In order that he might do this, he had first to take an examination which would require him to demonstrate that he had reached the educational standards expected of a fourteen-year-old. He duly passed the examination and was allowed to leave school. It was interesting for me to read many years later that, although in very different circumstances, the father of our former prime minister, Edward Heath, had also taken a similar examination in order that he might leave school early.

In the event, the only job open to my father in 1908 which would allow him to earn a little money was that of a van boy in the cartage section of the Great Western Railway (GWR). The next few years were very difficult for the entire remaining family, but were particularly tough for my father and his eldest sister, who, as I mentioned earlier, was close to him in age. Whilst they all went short of proper nutrition during this period, these two were at a vital stage in their growing cycles and this deprivation resulted in their being, in adult life, considerably smaller than their siblings. I can remember my father telling me that his abiding memory of those years was of always feeling hungry. By the time that the First World War (WW1) began in 1914, the family's situation had improved appreciably. At least two of his sisters had started work and were earning money, and his mother was doing her bit by taking in lodgers. The only member of the family who had been relatively unaffected by the initial change in the family's fortune was my Uncle Frank who, as a serving regular soldier, had naturally continued to be well fed and, as a result, had grown to be considerably taller than his brothers.

At the outbreak of the First World War in early August 1914, my father was working as a driver of horse-drawn vehicles for the GWR. My uncle Jack, however, had joined the Territorial Army in about 1912, and, as a result, he was mobilised immediately and, as a member of the 'contemptible little army' (the Kaiser's description), was present at its initial engagement at Mons, Belgium. My father was also keen to enlist, but he first needed to ensure that the family would be able to cope financially during his absence. Having satisfied himself on that score, he joined up in late 1914 or, possibly, early 1915. When he volunteered for army service, he was asked whether he was used to handling horses. He replied in the affirmative, and was then told that he would be enlisted into the Royal Artillery as a driver. His army records indicate that he arrived in France in June 1915, and he subsequently spent almost four years in both France and Belgium until he was eventually demobilised in 1919. During this period, he took part in all of the British Army's major engagements on the Western Front. When he was not towing big guns into position, he was frequently used in the transport of supplies and munitions to the front lines. Whilst engaged in the latter activity during the battle of the Somme in 1916, an enemy shell landed nearby and he was blown off his wagon. On recovering consciousness, he realised that he was lying in a shell hole and had wounds to his back and the back of his neck. These, fortunately, were not too serious and he made a quick recovery, but he was devastated to learn that his favourite horse had been killed! More serious to his long-term health was the effect of the poison gas that he experienced on another occasion, which would manifest itself much later.

Miraculously, all three Kemp brothers survived the First World War. I am not certain whether or not Uncle Frank, who was in the Indian Army, served on the Western Front, but he certainly took part in the vicious Mesopotamia (modern-day Iraq) campaign against one of the Central Powers, the Ottoman Empire. Although a side-show compared with the scale of the conflict in France and Belgium, the conditions were appalling, and the campaign involved a heavy defeat (the surrender and capture of General Townshend and his starving forces at Kut) and an eventual triumph (the rout of the Turkish forces and the capture of Baghdad by General Maude). General Maude did not live long to enjoy his victory, as, remarkably, both he and the opposing commander, the German General von der Golze, succumbed to cholera. Around 90,000 British and Indian lives were lost during the campaign, but the Turkish losses were in excess of 200,000; losses which must have seriously eroded their ability to prosecute the war in other theatres.

My father first met my mother when he went home on leave during WW1 and found that his mother had taken in a new lodger! They quickly formed a relationship, and married shortly after his demobilisation in 1919. By the mid-1930s, my father, who for as long as I can remember was keenly interested in both international and internal politics, was certain that another world war was on the way. In about 1935 at around the time that the Italians invaded Abyssinia (modern-day Ethiopia) he joined a territorial fusilier regiment, the 7th City of London Fusiliers (the 'shiny' seventh). How he managed to join is something of a mystery, as he was already showing signs of the lung damage that he had sustained during WW1. I can only presume that the army authorities failed to give him a thorough medical examination. A younger brother of my mother's, my uncle Tom, was already a member of the same territorial unit, and the two brothers-in-law were thus able to serve together. A year or two later the unit was converted from a fusilier regiment into Royal Engineers. Dad had an abortive call-up in 1938 during the Munich crisis, and was again called up in 1939 about two weeks before the outbreak of the Second World War (WW2), when he was exactly twelve days short of his forty-fifth birthday. He was keen to renew his acquaintance with France and attempted to get himself posted to the British Expeditionary Force, but the army turned this request down flat. Instead, he was stationed in Suffolk, where he spent much of the time driving an army lorry around and delivering supplies to a number of camps. After the British Army's collapse and the Dunkirk evacuation in 1940, conditions deteriorated appreciably. There was an imminent threat of invasion, and in the severe winter of 1940/41 he was often required to sleep at night in his army lorry. This had an injurious effect on his already fragile health, and he became seriously ill. Eventually, in about early August 1941, he was discharged from the army on medical grounds. Before he was released from the army, my father was presented with a document which he was told to sign. This document stated, amongst other information, that my father's illness had been aggravated by his war service. On reading this, my father told the officer who had presented the document that he was unable to sign it, as he objected to the term 'aggravated'. This infuriated the officer who tried to browbeat him into signing it with remarks like, 'Sign it, man'. However, like the good old artilleryman that he was, Dad stuck to his guns and told the officer politely but firmly that until the word 'aggravated' was removed and replaced by 'caused' he would not be signing anything. The officer had little choice but to comply, and my father left the army with a fifty per cent disability pension; an amount that was, after a number of years and numerous medical examinations, raised progressively to a hundred per cent.

My mother, as I will relate shortly, had died a few weeks before my father's discharge from the army, and Dad and I were alone together for the remainder of the war. We followed all of the subsequent wartime campaigns assiduously with the aid of wall maps and small paper flags that could be pinned on to the maps to indicate the movements of the opposing forces. Towards the latter part of 1941 and after a period of recovery, Dad was well enough to resume his occupation with the GWR as a 'Scammell' driver. Scammells (named, I believe, after the manufacturer) were the articulated vehicles that the GWR had adopted when they began to phase out horse-drawn vehicles in the 1920s. They consisted of a powerful cabin (usually referred to as the cab) that had a pivoting joint in the rear, which permitted it to tow and manoeuvre a large trailer. My father had been amongst the first GWR employees to drive one of these lorries. I am not sure of the precise date that he started this work, but it must have preceded the introduction of driving tests as I know that he was never required to take such a test. It was heavy and arduous work, and in pre-WW2 days he could count upon the assistance of a van boy. However, when, following his army discharge, he returned to his work, he found that van boys had been largely replaced by van girls; young women who, with the best will in the world, simply lacked the physical strength of the young men whom they replaced. This, of course put an additional strain upon the drivers, but he somehow managed to cope.

During the remaining war years, although, to a certain extent, my father and I led separate lives, I accompanied him regularly to the Finsbury Park Empire and other London theatres. He had always loved the old London music halls, and it was a pleasure to join him in his visits to theatres where we saw revivals of shows like *Chu Chin Chow* and *The Maid of the Mountains* as well as variety performances and Ivor Novello productions. By the mid1950s, my father had remarried, and his life had returned to a more contented and even keel. At around the same time, increasing ill health had obliged him to give up his cartage work, and he was given an office job with the GWR. He continued to work well into his late sixties, and, with a wife to accompany him, was able at last to travel overseas on holidays from time to time.

In his later years, Dad and his wife, Katherine (known as Kit), managed to buy a small house in East London where they lived for a number of years (the only time in his life when he owned property of any kind), but the house was compulsorily purchased by the council for a road-widening scheme and the pittance that they received in compensation did not allow them to buy a replacement. Dad spent the final years of his life in a reasonably comfortable council flat in Maidstone, Kent. His main concern towards the end was for Kit, who had suffered a serious injury in a road accident. I told him that I would keep in touch with her, and that I would ensure that she was well looked after. He was delighted to hear my pledge, and told me that I had set his mind to rest. Dad finally passed away, at the age of seventy-seven years, in November 1971.

Albert Kemp

Turning to my mother, she was born in Bethnal Green, London, in March 1898, and was the daughter of George Francis Spong and Matilda Hannah Spong (née Russell). She was christened Emma Sarah, and she had two older siblings named George and Matilda and five younger ones, sisters Caroline and Louise and brothers Thomas, James and John. I believe that there were two or more additional children originally, but they had died in infancy. Although she rarely talked about her early days, it seems that it was a somewhat dysfunctional family and she left home to strike out on her own when she was still in her teens. Before leaving home, Mum had been the victim of a rather bizarre accident. Her father, not normally violent, could become bad-tempered under the influence of drink, and during one such episode he, losing self-control completely, picked up a chair and threw it across the room. Unfortunately, my mother walked into the room at the same moment, and the chair struck her on the head and knocked her unconscious. I am not certain about the medical treatment that she might have received, if any, but the incident was certainly serious and quite possibly caused the grave illness that she suffered from later during her short life.

After leaving home, my mother continued to visit her parents and, as far as I am aware, remained on good terms with the other family members. However, as they all grew older, contacts with her siblings, with the exception of Tom and John, grew increasingly infrequent. It was not that she had fallen out with any of the others, but simply that she had more in common with Tom and, to a lesser extent, John. Tom, in particular, she had a high regard for. She and he had similar aspirations and were very much on the same wavelength. He, too, had left home at an early age and had for a time lodged with my parents until he was able to make his own way. John, the youngest member of the family, was unable to obtain regular work for many years, and my mother felt sorry for him and wanted to help him as much as possible. At the age of about seven or eight, I, at Mum's wish, started to take piano lessons, and I continued to do this for about four years until the outbreak of war in September 1939. My aptitude for the piano was reasonably good, and I had a decent touch which enabled me to colour melodies quite well. Whilst I would never have become an outstanding pianist (my fingers were quite short and stubby), I believe that I would have become fairly competent if the war had not intervened. Mum was keen to display my progress to relatives when visiting them in pre-war days (they normally had a piano if little else), and I was usually armed on such occasions with a satchel full of music with which I could give an impromptu 'recital'. If there was a popular song that she particularly liked, she would occasionally buy the sheet music and ask me to play it for her. Two such pieces that I recall were 'Harbour Lights' and 'Smoke gets in your Eyes'.

By the early 1930s when I was quite young, there were increasing concerns about changes in my mother's appearance and the fact that she was often unwell. She underwent a full medical examination, and it was eventually discovered that she had a tumour on the pituitary gland which, as my father described to me at the time, was just below the brain. Some time had elapsed before her malady was diagnosed as the condition had been extremely rare in Britain, but it is known nowadays as Cushing's syndrome. It was distorting her features and body shape and causing her to age prematurely. I believe that the pituitary gland can be operated on today, but this was not possible in my mother's time. This meant that she had, in effect, received a slow and lingering death sentence; a fact that, although I understood that she was very ill, was largely concealed from me at this period. Within a few months of the beginning of WW2, Mum and I were alone together at home. My brother, who was nineteen, had joined the Royal Navy (RN), and, by 1940, was undergoing training at the HMS Ganges shore establishment in Suffolk. He was, of course, of prime military age, and even if he had not volunteered, he would very soon have been conscripted. I had been evacuated to Northamptonshire a few days before the outbreak of war, but when the expected bombing of London failed to materialise, I had returned to London after about six weeks. I knew that I would be needed to assist my mother at home, particularly with the shopping as she was becoming increasingly immobile. There was, of course, no possibility that I could attend school – schools were all closed anyway.

We managed to cope together quite well until the Blitz on London began on 7 September 1940, when life, as I will explain later, got a lot more difficult. Suffice it to say for now that when the bombs were falling all around on a nightly basis, Mum was magnificent. She was concerned, of course, but her concern was for me – not for herself. In late June 1941, I was with her when she suffered a massive stroke. She had somehow managed to get dressed, and had gone into the kitchen in an attempt to do some baking. I, who was in another room, suddenly heard her calling and went to the kitchen. In very calm and matter-of-fact tones, she told me that there was something wrong with her and that she was dropping everything. She asked me to help her to get back into the bedroom and into bed, and to then seek medical assistance. I helped her as best I could, and then made my way to our doctor's surgery. Fortunately, I was able to contact the doctor immediately, and he returned with me to our home. After a brief examination, he realised that she needed to be hospitalised without delay and made the necessary arrangements. She suffered further strokes in hospital, and was unconscious when I last saw her. Mum passed away on 12 July 1941 at the age of forty-three years. She had always had a strong personality and an indomitable spirit, and had borne her affliction with great fortitude and stoicism.

I will now say a little more about my brother, Harry. As I mentioned earlier, after joining the Royal Navy he was sent to HMS Ganges to undergo his initial training. This training was, unfortunately, interrupted when he was sentenced to one month in the naval glasshouse for striking an NCO. However, after serving his time he completed his initial training, and was then posted to a gunnery school in North Wales. He achieved high ratings at this establishment, and was then assigned to a little-known part of the Royal Navy whose members carried the letters DEMS (Defensively Equipped Merchant Ship) on their hatbands. These naval personnel (known as the dems) were Royal Navy gunners on merchant ships. This work had during the early part of WW2 been undertaken by the army (the soldiers were known as the maritime artillery), but the responsibility was soon taken over by the Royal Navy. Anyone who has any knowledge about the casualty rate suffered by merchant ships during WW2 will recognise that it was an extremely dangerous area to serve in.

I am not certain whether or not it was the first vessel that he served on, but in early 1941 he joined a British tramp steamer of 5,961 tons, the SS Nirpura (see photo on page 29). He subsequently spent about two years on the Nirpura (mainly in the Far East and the Pacific) and had numerous narrow escapes after Japan entered the war. When the Japanese occupied Burma and entered Rangoon, about forty ships that were in the harbour, including the Nirpura, made desperate dashes for safety. These ships were sitting ducks for the Japanese Air Force, which enjoyed air superiority at the time, and the great majority of them were sent to the bottom of the sea. The Nirpura was one of just a tiny number that made it to safety and reached India. A bomb had, I was told, fallen into the Nirpura's funnel but had failed to explode, and was successfully defused at an Indian port. During the remainder of 1942, the Nirpura operated mainly in the Pacific theatre, transporting supplies, weapons and animals to Australian and other forces operating in places like New Guinea. Harry spent some time in Australia, where, amongst other things, he treated himself to a new civilian suit. By February 1943, the Nirpura had made its way to Durban, South Africa, and it was there that Harry left the Nirpura in order to return to the UK for some home leave.

Albert Kemp

In Durban, in late February 1943, he boarded the Canadian Pacific liner, Empress of Canada, a 21,517-ton vessel which had been requisitioned and converted for use as a troopship in 1939 (see photo on page 29). Including the crew, around 1,800 persons were reported to have been on board the liner on 1 March 1943, when, bound for the UK via Takoradi in West Africa, it departed from Durban. Among the 1,346 passengers were a large number of Greek and Polish refugees, about 500 Italian prisoners of war (POWs) and 50 Royal Navy personnel (including my brother). After a brief stop in Cape Town, the liner continued into the South Atlantic and was about four hundred miles south of Cape Palmas, Liberia, when it was attacked by an Italian submarine, the Leonardo da Vinci. A torpedo struck the Empress of Canada shortly after midnight on 13 March 1943, and the Italian commander of the submarine gave Captain Gould, the liner's commander, half an hour to abandon ship. He then fired a second torpedo into the stricken vessel, which sank about twenty minutes later. Harry and the other RN personnel were still on the liner when it received the second torpedo, having been instructed to remain on deck and await further orders. By this time, most of the lifeboats had been launched, and, realising that the ship would soon go down, the RN lads made their way to the last remaining lifeboats.

Harry and a few mates managed to get into a lifeboat and away from the Empress of Canada before it sank, but the lifeboat was grossly overcrowded and it turned over during the night. As the lifeboat turned turtle, Harry dived clear of the lifeboat to avoid being trapped underneath it and then held on to the upturned lifeboat until daybreak. As dawn arrived, he realised that only about ten of the lifeboat's original occupants were still around. These included a few crewmembers, a Polish lady and two of his naval friends. With the help of others, Harry somehow managed to get the Polish lady on to the top of the upturned lifeboat. Other people were also attempting to clamber onto the lifeboat. My brother and his friends, however, had spotted another lifeboat in the distance, and they decided to try to swim to it. They were now beginning to get the unwelcome attention of small sharks, and they realised that they would have to make the swim as quickly as possible. As they approached the other lifeboat, they were recognised by naval personnel who called out in encouragement. Harry told me that when he was about thirty yards from the lifeboat, he had looked around to see where his friends were, and seen fins sticking up out of the water. He realised that he had to make a final spurt, and, as he put it, he 'beat Johnny Weissmuller' (the famous Olympian swimmer) to the boat. A second friend also made it to safety, but the third member of the trio was not so lucky. He was a less powerful swimmer than the others, and in the final stages of the swim he had been badly bitten. Although he reached the lifeboat and was pulled aboard, he bled to death in the boat.

Before the Empress of Canada sank, its wireless operator had been able to put out SOS signals. Allied seaplanes were soon on the scene, and naval vessels were rushed to the area. About three and a half days after the submarine attack, an RN ship rescued Harry and the other survivors from their lifeboat and took them to an American base in Freetown, Sierra Leone, where Harry was given some temporary naval clothing. He had, of course, lost everything that he had been hoping to take back to the UK, including his Australian suit! Most of the other survivors from the liner had already been rescued and taken to Freetown before he arrived there. He was pleased to learn later that the Polish lady and the other people whom he had last seen on the upturned lifeboat were among the survivors. Altogether, almost four hundred of the people who had sailed from South Africa in the Empress of Canada were lost due to drowning, exposure and sharks. Ironically, in view of the fact that the attack on the liner had been made by an Italian submarine, the heaviest casualties proportionately in any national group occurred amongst the Italian POWs. The sinking of the Empress of Canada was the first of the successes achieved by the Leonardo da Vinci during its mission to hunt Allied vessels in South African waters, and, over the next two and a half months in the South Atlantic and the Indian Ocean, it claimed five further victims. It was the most successful war patrol made by any Italian submarine in WW2, and its Captain, Lt Gianfranco Gazzana-Priaroggia, was decorated and promoted. However, on its way back to its base in Bordeaux, France, the submarine made a fatal error. On 22 May 1943, it radioed that it was returning home, and the signal was intercepted and the submarine's position and direction fixed by Allied direction-finding equipment. On the following day, the Leonardo da Vinci was subjected to an intensive depth-charge attack by RN warships, the destroyer HMS Active and the frigate HMS Ness, and it sank with the loss of everyone on board.

As far as the Nirpura was concerned, it, too, had left Durban on about 1 March 1943, and had been bound for Karachi with thirty-nine members of the South African Defence Force and eight hundred mules on board when it was torpedoed and sunk by the German U-boat, U-160, on 3 March 1943 when only about two days out from Durban. I believe that Harry might have received this information when he was in Freetown, but in any case he knew by the time he got back to the UK that he had been destined to be sunk regardless of whether he had remained on the Nirpura or transferred to the Empress of Canada. My father and I, of course, had known nothing about his ordeal until he arrived home on leave, but we did have a prior inkling that something had gone wrong when my father received a telegram from Durban asking whether Harry was safe, and signed, it appeared, by three ladies!

Reproduced below, is a photograph of the SS Nirpura; a vessel on which Harry served as a Royal Navy gunner for two years.

Here is a photograph of the RMS Empress of Canada; the one on which my brother was returning to the UK for home leave when it was torpedoed in mid-Atlantic in March 1943. I believe that at least three ships have borne this illustrious name.

After an extensive shore leave, Harry was posted to a tanker and travelled in it to the USA, where it was filled up with aviation spirit. The tanker then joined a convoy that was bound for Italy. Whilst in the Atlantic, the convoy suffered ferocious attacks by U-boat packs and lost a number of vessels. Later, after passing through the straits of Gibraltar, enemy aircraft also took part in the assault on the convoy. When a ship laden with aviation spirit was hit by enemy fire, Harry told me, it would often explode and develop into a giant torch. He said he had seen more than one such catastrophe. In the event, his ship made it safely to an Italian port, and unloaded its dangerous cargo. During the last two years of the war, he made many more such voyages in various ships –these included at least one more trip to the USA and taking part in the D-Day landings in June 1944, when he made repeated journeys to the invasion beaches. Another vessel on which he was serving, the name of which I did not obtain, was sunk whilst in port by enemy aircraft. When WW2 came to an end, Harry received five campaign medals and two clasps. Harry suffered from vascular dementia during the final stage of his life, and died in February 2006, at the age of eighty-five years. His eldest son Michael, who took care of his medals after his death, has mounted his decorations in a display cabinet.

Chapter 3

My Early Life and Parental Influences

Now, I think that I should write a little more about my rather unusual childhood, my parental influences and my early life in the workplace and in the Services. The first school that I attended for a few months at the age of four was an infant school in Mowlem Street, Bethnal Green, close to where we were living in Cambridge Heath. However, my parents had, for some considerable time, had their names down for a place in the Sutton Dwellings development at the corner of City Road and Old Street, Shoreditch. In early 1932 a vacancy was offered to them, and we duly moved into 7 C block, Sutton Dwellings; a move which was particularly beneficial to my father as it put him within walking distance of his workplace at Smithfield. Our development, which had been constructed in 1911, was one of a number of such developments in London established by the Sutton Dwellings Trust, which had been founded under the will of their benefactor, William Richard Sutton; a self-made multi-millionaire who wanted to provide good accommodation for the deserving poor of London. William Sutton died in May 1900, but work on his projects was delayed by problems connected with his will, which was strongly contested by relatives. Nevertheless, the first development in Bethnal

Green was completed in 1909, and the City Road/Old Street development was the second one to be built. Several others in Chelsea, Rotherhithe, Islington and North Kensington followed, and in the 1920s and 1930s the Trust extended its operations to other large cities. As far as I am aware, the Chelsea development is the only London development still standing. Some London developments would, of course, have been heavily bombed during WW2. Although somewhat primitive by modern standards (the bath situated in the kitchen of each flat doubled as a kitchen table), the flats were well constructed, reasonably warm and completely free of mice and other vermin; assets that could not be claimed for most of the properties available in the 1930s to the poorer London residents. At some time in the mid-1930s, we moved from 7 C Block into the flat at 15 I Block (probably because it was larger).

Before going into details about my formal education, I would like to mention two examples of parental influences that come to mind. The first of these occurred in the summer of 1939, shortly after we had moved away from Sutton Dwellings. Whilst exploring my new home area, I hopped on a bus to visit Clissold Park, which was just a short distance away. While walking through the park in a grassy area, I noticed two boys about two hundred yards away who were squaring up to each other and obviously about to have a fight. This in itself was not too unusual, but the fact that one of the boys was black was certainly very unusual. Walking parallel with me but about twenty yards away to my right were two young white boys of about nine or ten years who, noticing that hostilities were about to start, immediately started to scream out, 'Come on –the white boy.' This annoyed me, as they were taking sides purely on racial grounds and clearly had no idea about the cause of the fight. As a counter to their action, I decided on the spur of the moment to call out, 'Come on –the one who didn't start it.' When it began, the fight was something of a fiasco, as, after a brief spell of sparring, the black boy landed a right hand which flattened the white boy, and then slowly walked away. I cannot emphasise enough just how rare it was to see a black youngster at that time. In fact, the only black person whom I remember seeing occasionally when I was young was the famous black tipster known as Prince Monolulu who frequented crowded places such as Club Row, London, on a Sunday morning and walked around murmuring, 'I got a horse.' An individual would approach him from time to time and money could be seen to change hands in exchange for a slip of paper. The other example occurred when I was about fifteen years old, and, together with six other lads, made my way to Hackney Marshes where we hoped to have a game of football. When we arrived in the area where we hoped to play, we saw, to our surprise, a group of nine Jewish youngsters of about the same age who were there for the same purpose. A couple of our own group were rather hostile at first, but I intervened and said something like, 'There aren't enough of us to have a decent game of football. Why don't we ask them if they would like to have a game with us.' This idea was agreed, and I approached the Jewish lads and put our proposal to them. They immediately accepted our offer, and, as they had an advantage in numbers, one of them offered to referee the match. This impromptu match was a great success, and both sides thoroughly enjoyed it. The referee controlled the match with scrupulous fairness, and when one of his group complained about the award of a free kick to our side, he dealt with him very firmly. These ideas about fair play and the need to avoid racial prejudice were unlikely, in my opinion, to be innate, and were almost certainly formed from comments made by my parents.

My early years in the infant/junior school in Cranwood Street (just outside Sutton Dwellings) were highly successful, and I came top of the class in the yearly examinations on several occasions. I had been able to read and write well at an early age, and my father, recognising that I was particularly interested in history and geography, began to acquire books for me. He could not afford to buy new books, but his daily walks to and from work took him past a bookstall which sold second-hand books at a tiny fraction of their original price. One day, when I was about six or seven years old, he came home with two encyclopedias that seemed practically brand new. They were entitled *The Wonderland of Knowledge*, and I spent ages poring over them and using them as reference sources. Through them, I was able to obtain a good knowledge of ancient Greek and Roman history, as well as much other useful information. The encyclopedias were intended for children, but their tone and content were quite adult, and I was amazed many years later to see how relatively childish similar books had become. Ominous signs that everything was not going to be plain sailing arrived, however, in 1934, when I had two spells in hospital with scarlet fever and diphtheria. Bacterial illnesses were rife in Central London in the 1930s, and, in those pre-antibiotic days, difficult to treat. Scarlet fever was not taken too seriously (almost all children had it at one time or another), but diphtheria was another matter. Official figures show that around one third of the young children who caught diphtheria did not survive. I spent about eight weeks with it in a North London hospital and during that time I was not permitted to see my parents. I have a very vague recollection of something being inserted into my throat (possibly a breathing tube of some kind).

After my discharge from hospital, I continued to do well at school, but by 1936/1937 I was having acute chest problems and, accompanied by my mother, was being obliged to spend much time visiting hospitals as an outpatient. Eventually, in early 1938, I had a chest x-ray which revealed that I had scarring and tubercular cells on the lungs. I was immediately rushed into the Royal Free Hospital, where I was placed in a tuberculosis ward. During a stay in the ward of about five weeks I had around seven or eight x-rays, at the end of which it was thought that the tubercular cells on my lungs were no longer active. I was then released into a convalescent home in Folkestone for a few weeks. After leaving the convalescent home, it was decided that I needed to attend an open air school, and arrangements were made for me to go to Holly Court School, Hampstead, for one year. Such schools were in vogue at this time (early summer, 1938) for youngsters who had experienced severe chest ailments, and were designed to improve their health and well-being as well as provide an education (see the note and photographs on page 36). Attending Holly Court school involved my travelling daily by tram (later trolleybus) from City Road to the terminus at Highgate Village and then walking about a half or three-quarters of a mile to the school, and to make the reverse journey later. I am sure that the teaching staff at the school did their best, but with dual objectives to meet (education and health improvement) compromises were inevitable. Our curriculum included frequent walks around Hampstead Heath, physical training and gardening (attending to the school allotments), as well as normal school lessons. We also did a lot of singing (presumably to exercise our lungs) and, mainly in the early stages of my time there, had occasional rest periods. It is surprising that I can still remember some of the songs that we used to sing. They included 'Old Father Thames', 'The Gay Highway' and 'Marching through Georgia'. The last-named may have been introduced by an American exchange teacher whom we had for a short time. When I started at Holly Court, I was placed in class 2 among children who were slightly older, but after about four months I took an annual examination and came top. I was then put into class 1 (the highest class), where some of the children were as much as two years older. When I left the school in the early summer of 1939 and after I had completed my year there, I was certainly in much better physical condition but it had not done a great deal for my general education. I had certainly not received anything like an adequate preparation for examinations like, for example, the eleven-plus.

Shortly after I left Holly Court, we moved away from Sutton Dwellings to a house in Balmes Road (just inside the borough of Hackney). The

The photographs of Holly Court Open Air school above were furnished by the London Metropolitan Archives. The upper one illustrates the distinctive wooden structures that served as classrooms, whilst the lower one shows the school's main building. The grounds included a sports field and an asphalted games area, as well as extensive allotments in which the pupils helped to grow the vegetables needed for their lunchtime meals. I am not certain of the precise period when the use of such schools was discontinued, but when antibiotics became available soon after WW2 their need, I imagine, was considerably diminished.

move had been necessitated by my mother's worsening medical state, and her consequent inability to negotiate the stairs to and from our top-floor flat in Sutton Dwellings. A school had to be found for me, and the only one that I could attend at that time was the Pitfield Street Secondary School for boys. Before starting at this school, my father, who wanted me to attend the Northern Polytechnic, Holloway, had a lengthy talk with the headmaster at Pitfield Street School. They apparently discussed my case in considerable detail, and a joint decision was made to the effect that, provided that I continued to make good progress, arrangements would be made for me to join the Northern Polytechnic when I was thirteen. In the event, I only spent around two to three months at Pitfield Street School, and my time there was not a happy one. The treatment of the pupils at this school was far worse than I had ever seen at previous schools, and the viciousness with which punishments were given on almost a daily basis had to be witnessed to be believed. The teachers, who appeared to be mainly from the provinces, seemed to imagine that the pupils were little more than savages who could only be controlled if the teachers instituted a reign of terror. Whilst it was true that the school was situated in a tough neighbourhood, most of the pupils were more than ready to learn and behave properly if given half a chance. The very few who did conform to the teachers' stereotypes were rarely caned themselves but were quite adept at getting other youngsters into trouble; usually the ones who were less bright and more easily led. It was almost a relief when, on 1 September 1939, and the declaration of war was imminent, I was evacuated to Northamptonshire. My short spell at Pitfield Street School had produced in me a lifelong opponent of corporal punishment.

After I returned to London about six weeks later, I found that all the local schools were closed and I devoted myself to helping my mother. I took over the shopping completely, and, armed with a shopping list provided by Mum, went out regularly to buy the food that we needed. We had to obtain food on most days as, like the great majority of households in the UK at this time, we had no refrigeration. I also tackled most of the housework, but Mum did pay the woman who lived in our upstairs rooms to carry out tasks that she thought might be beyond my capabilities. By late October 1939 I had reached the age of twelve and, although I realised that I was being massively disadvantaged by not being able to attend school, I did my best to compensate for this by continuing to read widely in my spare time. When the Blitz started in early September 1940, there were no air raid shelters available in our immediate neighbourhood. A modern factory at the top of our road (called something like the Texryte) made its basement areas available as night shelters, but there was no way that Mum could have taken advantage of them and we had to remain in our house and hope for the best. Even the mice in our house were terrified, and could be heard running up and down inside some fixed indoor shutters whenever bombs landed nearby. I, too, as time passed, was becoming increasingly nervous (although trying desperately not to show it), and probably exhibiting signs of sleep deprivation. After about five or six weeks of nightly bombing, Dad came home on leave for a short period, and the day before he was due to return to his unit he said to me, 'By the way, you are coming with me to Suffolk tomorrow. I have arranged accommodation for you in a village just outside Stowmarket, and for you to go to a school in Stowmarket.' I was taken aback to hear this, and replied, 'I can't do that, Dad. Who is going to look after Mum?' 'Don't worry about that,' he said. 'Your grandfather will be here tomorrow, and he will take care of her.' Sure enough, the old chap turned up on the following morning with his suitcase, and I left for Suffolk with my father. In retrospect, I realised that my parents, in the correspondence that passed between them at this time, must have discussed my situation and decided that I needed to get away from the bombing. It is likely, too, that they were influenced by the fact that I had not been able to get to school for over a year.

I quite enjoyed the seven months that I spent in Suffolk, although I missed my mother acutely. The Stowmarket school regime was far more civilised than the earlier London ones that I had known, and the classes included both boys and girls (a situation that I hadn't experienced since infant school). Additionally, it was good to be away from the bombing for a while. In this more relaxed atmosphere, I caught up quickly and made good progress. On one occasion in class, after studying ancient civilisations for several weeks, we were all required to write an essay on the history of the Sumerians. A day or two later, our teacher told us that she had read all of the essays and considered two of them to be outstanding –she referred to the one that I had produced and one written by another boy. She added that both essays were excellent, but thought that my one had a slight edge. In May 1941, my father contacted me and told me that it was necessary that I return to London as soon as possible. My grandfather, it seemed, was no longer able to take care of Mum, as the strain had eventually become too great, and he was now unwell himself. I returned to London with my father, and was shocked by my mother's appearance when I saw her again. She had great difficulty in getting to her feet when I entered the room where she was situated, and looked like a little, very old, lady. We were, nevertheless, delighted to see each other again, and I soon got back to my 'caring' routine. The air raids were now much more intermittent, and it was easier for me to get around on my shopping expeditions. The strokes that she suffered, recounted earlier, that put an end to Mum's short life, began about five weeks after my return. I was grateful for the opportunity that I had received to see her again if only for a short time, and will never forget the courage that she showed during this final phase of her life.

Some time later, I cannot remember precisely when, Dad told me that before I left Suffolk, he had been called in to see the headmaster at my school, who had entreated him not to take me back to London. Dad had replied that he had no wish to take me back, but really had no choice as my mother had lost her carer and had very little time to live. Dad had not told me this at the time, as he did not wish to unsettle me. What would have happened if I had remained at the school, I really have no idea, but I know that some of the youngsters at the school with whom I played football during our lunchtime breaks were fifteen years of age and in higher classes, and must, therefore, have been receiving a good level of education. When I reached the age of fourteen in October 1941, a few of the inner London schools were beginning to reopen, but from the enquiries that my father made it seemed that there was no possibility of my attending one for a lengthy period. I had no choice, therefore, but to look for employment. There was very little of this available for a young lad with no qualifications, and my father suggested that I start at the bottom in the General Post Office (GPO) as a boy messenger and try to work my way up. I agreed to do this, and was accepted by the GPO and assigned to the main post office in Upper Street, Islington, in the N1 district of London. I worked as a boy messenger delivering telegrams for about two years, and, although I disliked the work, it was not without its benefits. The N1 district in which we made our deliveries was divided into three parts for delivery purposes, and covered a considerable part of Central London. To allow us to carry out our work over appreciable distances the boy messengers were each provided with a bicycle, and the daily cycling regimes were certainly good for my general health. Another benefit was an interesting piece of social information that I received. I found, when making my deliveries, that the rougher, tougher and more deprived the area, the more generous the people were! Earning a wage of just sixteen shillings for a six-day week, tips were naturally welcome, and no area was better at providing these than the tough Hoxton district. Time and again when delivering there, after allowing the recipient (often a little old lady) to peruse the contents of the telegram and turning to go, I would hear something like, 'No, wait sonny.' The person would then disappear into the house and return a few moments later with a three-penny tip. I was touched by the generosity of these people, who, I was sure, could ill afford to make such payments. It was a humbling and enlightening experience, and one that I have never forgotten.

At the age of fifteen, I started to attend the GPO school twice a week as a preparatory course for the boy messengers' examination that I would take at sixteen. This school was surprisingly good, and while it did not, for example, delve into higher mathematics it had a fairly broad curriculum which included some very useful writing practices. One such practice that I recall doing quite frequently would require us to read a passage of about two or three thousand words and then summarise it in around four hundred words. As far as I can recall, roughly two hundred of us took the examination in late 1943, and the top twenty (which included myself) were interviewed for sixteen counter clerk vacancies. I was one of the four rejects (possibly because I was considered to be too small), and was one of the next thirty-four boys who were to become telegraphists. The remaining hundred and fifty were divided, according to their examination positions, into sorters and postmen. The counter clerks and telegraphists started their respective training courses immediately, but the lower hundred and fifty remained messengers until they were eighteen years of age. Eight youngsters (males and females) including myself took part in the telegraphist training course that I attended, and one of the skills that we had to acquire was to be able to touch-type proficiently. The typewriters on which we practised had purpose-built raised key covers, which enabled us to type without being able to see the keys. The piano-playing activities that I had undertaken before the war gave me an advantage over the other youngsters, as my fingers were used to seeking out piano keys and were consequently more nimble. As a result, I started to get too far ahead, and had to be slowed down! Once we had become reasonably proficient, we graduated to the GPO teleprinters. These were superb machines which possessed two space bars, and on which one could, with practice, develop tremendous speeds. The Royal Signals teleprinters, which I used for a time during my army service, were not in the same class.

I quite enjoyed my work as a telegraphist during the final twenty months of WW2. We handled large amounts of military traffic (usually coded) at the Central Telegraph Office in London during this period as well as the normal traffic, and I felt that, if only in a very small way, I was doing something to assist the war effort. Such was the volume of traffic that telegraphic log-jams to certain destinations sometimes developed, and a few of us who could send a hundred messages per hour were frequently called upon to help clear the backlogs. For several days prior to 6 June 1944 (D-Day), we had realised from the increase in military traffic that an invasion was imminent. I was worried about D-Day initially, as I recognised the difficulties inherent in mounting such an operation. At about this time, I joined the Air Training Corps (Air Cadets), as I expected to be called up before the end of the war and my preference was for the Royal Air Force (RAF). Our meetings took place in a school building and covered subjects such as navigation and aircraft maintenance. These training sessions were frequently interrupted by air raid sirens, and such disturbances became increasingly prevalent during the V1 (Flying Bomb) period. On one occasion several of us went up on to the school's flat roof to get a better look at the bombs as they were approaching. It was dark at the time and with the flames coming out of the rear of their engines, they could be seen when still miles away. We watched several of the V1s as they passed by in the night sky, until their engines cut out and they plummeted to earth and triggered a loud explosion. It was a silly and foolhardy thing to do, and what precisely we would have done if we had seen a V1 heading straight towards us I do not know. Presumably, we would have made a mad dash for the stairs and tried to get down to the basement as soon as possible. A few months later, when London was under attack by the V2 rockets, we had no choice but to continue with our everyday lives, as these bombs landed without warning. On one occasion when I was on the upstairs deck of a bus and on my way to work, there was a huge explosion nearby and the blast from the bomb rocked the bus to and fro and almost caused it to fall over. I later learned that this V2 had fallen in an area full of early morning tradespeople, and that it had killed eighty of them.

After the war in Europe had come to an end in May 1945, I thought it probable that at least another twelve months would elapse before the war against Japan could be brought to a favourable conclusion. Bearing in mind the tenacity with which the Japanese had defended Okinawa and other islands, it was obvious that a successful seaborne invasion of the Japanese main islands, even for a nation as powerful as the USA, would be an enormous operation and would need considerable planning. It seemed likely, therefore, that I would be called up shortly after my eighteenth birthday in October 1945, and that I could well be involved in the operation with the British forces. I, of course, knew nothing about the development of the atomic bomb at this time, or that it was going to be used in the near future. As is well known, atomic bombs were dropped on Hiroshima and Nagasaki in late August 1945, and these terrible events brought WW2 to an end far earlier than I had expected (and provoked a moral dilemma that persists to this day). Whilst it is true that large numbers of people suffered horrific deaths, I have no doubt that a full-scale invasion of the Japanese homeland would have caused enormous casualties not only to the Allied forces but also to the Japanese forces and, above all, the civilian population of Japan. These casualties might well have run into many millions, and the Japanese infrastructure (already badly damaged) could have been virtually obliterated. Also, the importance of the concept of 'face' to far-eastern peoples needs to be taken into account. The dropping of the atomic bombs, awful though they were, gave the Japanese an opportunity to accept unconditional surrender without losing too much face. So was the use of atomic weapons the lesser of two evils, or was there an alternative strategy available which could have achieved the same objectives– the demilitarisation of Japan and its transformation into an important democratic nation? If a plausible alternative action could have been taken at the time, then I, for one, would be interested to hear about it. Finally, when reviewing the events that brought an end to WW2, the vital role played by Emperor Hirohito in persuading the Japanese people to accept unconditional surrender should be given the recognition and praise that it deserves. Cries by certain British journalists that Emperor Hirohito should have been prosecuted as a war criminal were, in my view, totally devoid of common sense, and are examples of idiocy at its most blatant. When WW2 finally came to an end, I, like most people, felt considerable relief that it was all over. When reviewing the events that had occurred in Europe during the war, my principal thought was that there had to be a better way for the countries of Europe to live together.

A few months after the end of the war, I was called to a pre-service interview in which I was asked about the part of the armed forces that I wished to join. In practice I was given little choice, as when I mentioned my ATC training and nominated the RAF the interviewer told me that the RAF had far more personnel than they needed and that it would have to be the army. I was called up in March 1946, and did my primary training at a camp near Retford, Nottinghamshire. After completing this phase I was assigned to the Royal Signals and posted to Catterick, where I trained as an OKL (operator keyboard and line). The 'line' part of the training involved learning how to transmit and receive messages efficiently using Morse code. After completing my training, which took several months, I spent a few weeks in a transit camp before being posted to the Middle East. I arrived at Alexandria in late December 1946 or early

January 1947, and was transported to another transit camp in a suburb of Cairo, where I remained for about two weeks. Whilst I was in this transit camp an officer, addressing the rank and file who were on parade, ordered all those serving in the Royal Signals who had trained as OKLs and had previously worked on GPO teleprinters to step forward. Six of the men present (including myself) met the required criteria and stepped forward. We were then told that we were going to be posted to various army HQs. Two were to stay at the HQ in Cairo, two were to go to the HQ at Ismailia and the final two (of whom I was one) were to go to HQ Palestine in Jerusalem. After travelling to Jerusalem by rail and road, my colleague and I were taken to our billets in the HQ Palestine camp in Allenby Barracks, which was sited on the Bethlehem Road just to the south of Jerusalem. There we learned that we would be required to make daily return journeys to an annexe in the King David Hotel complex in Jerusalem, where we would be working in the Royal Signals office.

I soon discovered the reason why I and my colleague had been allocated to HQ Palestine, rather than to the main Royal Signals unit in Jerusalem (close to Allenby Barracks) where I could have carried out the work for which I had been trained. Huge amounts of memoranda were being generated daily for circulation to army units throughout Palestine (around a hundred thousand troops were in Palestine at this time), and the army clerks (soldiers who had been given short clerical courses and rudimentary typing instruction) had shown themselves unable to cope with the volume and accuracy requirements. The memos had to be typed onto a foolscap stencil, which was then used to produce a large number of copies. I had no problem with being ordered to do this work, as it was clearly the army's prerogative to employ me in whatever capacity they thought would be most useful. A train of events that I did find objectionable, however, began roughly six months later when the Chief Clerk (a warrant officer who was i/c clerical staff) called me into his office. He told me that due to the demobilisation of the Signals HQ sergeant, a vacancy had arisen for a new non-commissioned officer (NCO) and that he would be recommending me for the position. He added, rather flatteringly, that he regarded me as by far the outstanding candidate for this promotion. I was naturally delighted to hear this, but my delight turned into dismay a few days later when the Chief Clerk called me back into his office and, very apologetically, told me that my promotion had been vetoed by none other than Brigadier (***** - I am withholding his name), the senior Royal Signals officer in Palestine, and, for all I know, the entire Middle East. The Brigadier would not hear of it, the Chief Clerk told me, as I was not a clerk! I was certain that there was nothing personal in the Brigadier's decision, as I doubt that he would have known me from Adam. He was obviously concerned that, if promoted, I would not be able to perform my typing marathons. Any such concern would have been entirely misplaced, as I was quite sure that I would have been able to combine the minimal supervisory duties needed with my typing work, if not 'standing on my head' at least very easily. The decision to use six of the best OKLs (men who had performed similar work in the GPO) in order to overcome typing deficiencies in HQs at Cairo, Ismailia and Jerusalem must have been made by, or at least authorised by, a very senior Royal Signals officer –possibly the Brigadier-General in Jerusalem. I have often wondered how the four men who were posted to Cairo and Ismailia fared, and whether they, too, were similarly disbarred from promotion. This episode left a very bad taste in my mouth, as it indicated that no matter how well I performed my duties there was no possibility that I could ever get promoted. The private who was promoted in my place (a friend of mine) moved up the ladder, as I had anticipated, as further demobilisations occurred, and was a sergeant by the time that I left Palestine about a year later.

During the first few months that I was in Palestine, I quite enjoyed my time there. We were able to move around fairly freely when off duty, and some of us used this opportunity to visit many of the famous biblical sites. There had been some terrorist activity in Jerusalem shortly before I arrived –notably the blowing up of a section of the King David Hotel –but travel to places like the Dead Sea, Jaffa and Nazareth was not too difficult initially. However, by about June/July 1947 conditions had deteriorated considerably, and we had to carry our firearms twenty-four hours a day and sleep on top of them (rifle under the palliasse) at night. One chap, in an adjoining hut, stood his rifle against the hut wall when he went to bed instead of under his palliasse, and it was stolen during the night. He was put on a charge, of course, and sentenced to a spell in the army glasshouse in Gaza. This fellow was exceptionally unlucky, as when making his return journey to Jerusalem, he was killed when the train on which he was travelling was blown up. Our sporting activities (notably football – we had a football pitch just outside the camp perimeter), which we had enjoyed in the early days, came to an end after a concealed explosive device (placed it was thought by the Irgun Zvei Leumi –a Jewish terrorist organisation) was found on our football pitch. For most of the time that I was in Palestine, we were unable to venture outside our camp unless we were armed and in a group of at least four people. The dangers involved in disregarding this order were highlighted when a Ceylonese man, serving in the British Army, who had ventured alone just outside the camp main gate was shot down and killed, apparently by Arabs who made off quickly with his rifle. I had befriended this chap, who had no compatriots serving with him, a few days earlier when I saw him alone in the camp canteen. He had seemed grateful to have somebody to talk to and spoke to me at length about his life in Ceylon (now known, of course, as Sri Lanka) and what had prompted him to join the British Army.

During the last six months of 1947 and the first six months of 1948, hostilities between the Arabs and the Jews in Palestine increased considerably and eventually became a full-scale war. Intelligence reports, to which I had access, indicated that atrocities were being committed by both sides, and that many people were being forced to leave their homes and seek refuge elsewhere amongst their own ethnic groups. I, and the other servicemen who worked in HQ buildings, continued to make our daily journeys to central Jerusalem, until, as a part of the British withdrawal process, we evacuated Jerusalem in April 1948 and moved to a new HQ in Haifa. I have seen accounts of the British withdrawal from Palestine on TV that suggest that all British forces left that country in April 1948. This is incorrect, as I did not leave Palestine until late June or early July 1948, and I was by no means amongst the last to go. I well remember the celebrations that took place in Haifa in May 1948, when the State of Israel came into existence. Together with a few of my comrades, I enjoyed a meal in an Israeli restaurant in Haifa during this period. Contacts with members of the local population during my time in Palestine were extremely rare, and as far as I personally was concerned, were largely confined to a handful of Christian Arabs who worked for the British Army in other parts of the King David Hotel Annexe.

The vessel that took me on the first part of my journey home for demobilisation went through the Suez Canal, and dropped me and my servicemen friends off at the town of Suez at the southern end of the Canal. There, we remained for about a week until we boarded the Staffordshire, a converted troopship which took us back through the Suez Canal and continued through the Mediterranean and into the Atlantic before eventually arriving in Liverpool. There, I went through the normal demobilisation procedures before returning home, where I was just in time to see, on one of the very early televisions, the London 1948 Olympic Games. So much leave was owed to me at this time (I had taken very little for almost two years) that my army service did not end officially until September 1948. Whilst enjoying this long spell of leave, I went to Lord's Cricket Ground, where I saw the famous Australian touring side of 1948 play Middlesex. Many members of this team, which included the one and only Don Bradman, were legends in their own lifetimes and with Denis Compton and Bill Edrich playing for Middlesex, it was a day to remember. It was a pity that my memories of my time in the army (which, as described earlier, had included a vetoed recommendation for promotion) were not happier, as, unlike many conscripts, I had been quite keen to serve in the armed forces. About five years after I had been demobbed, I received a letter from the army authorities recalling me for further training. It was in compliance with a government scheme of some kind (I cannot recall its purpose or the duration of the additional service), but by that time I was working for the Admiralty who, when they learned about the letter, wrote to the army and, it seems, told them to 'back off'. In any case, I received another letter from the army about a week later, which stated that owing to a change in occupation I was no longer subject to recall.

Towards the end of 1961, I transferred to the Home Office and began a lengthy spell of work in the Immigration Service. During this period, I took seven Civil Service foreign language examinations, and had comfortable passes in all of them. This was not quite as good as it sounds, as, due to the need to requalify within five years after passing a foreign language examination in order to retain one's language allowance, just three foreign languages were involved. Nevertheless, I did, during my stint in Immigration, pass French three times, Spanish twice and Turkish twice and had no failures; a decent effort, I think, from a fellow who never had an opportunity to learn a word of any foreign language during his schooldays.

Chapter 4

The Gathering Storm

We have now fast-forwarded to 2012, and I, of course, have been retired for many years and will, in the latter part of 2012, reach eighty-five years of age. A few years earlier, in 2008–2009, a banking crisis had been experienced in the UK which had started in the USA and had spread to other countries throughout the developed world. This undoubtedly was a serious setback for the UK, as a period of steady economic growth had been stopped in its tracks. However, whilst the crisis had certainly depleted our reserves it had not fundamentally changed the UK economy, and I was confident that the UK would soon make a full recovery and continue on its road to prosperity. There were encouraging signs of this in the middle of 2012 when, despite the financial restraints, the UK had been able to put on what I considered to be a magnificent Olympic Games. I was intensely proud of both the way that these games had been organised, and by the superb efforts of the British competitors. I also felt certain that most of the numerous overseas visitors who had come to the UK to enjoy the Olympic events at first hand would have taken away a favourable impression of our country.

Unfortunately, my comfortable ideas about the future prospects for the UK received a considerable shock on 23 January 2013, when Prime Minister David Cameron announced, in the course of a long speech about the EU and the UK's position in it, that he would allow a second referendum on the UK's membership to be held. I had previously held a high opinion of David Cameron, and had regarded him as one of the more decent Conservative politicians.   Consequently, I could hardly believe what I had heard, and his pledge to hold a referendum seemed a colossal and unnecessary error of judgement. I must confess that although I had felt obliged to take part in the 1975 referendum, I have always disliked referenda on principle. They represent, I believe, an abdication of governmental responsibilities, particularly when, as in this case, they concern matters of huge complexity and have massive ramifications. The Germans, I believe, had the right idea when, in the process of adopting their current constitution (one of the most truly democratic in the western world) they banned referenda completely. They had seen at first hand just how easy it had been for Hitler to gain approval through referenda for actions such as annexing Austria and leaving the League of Nations.

I could understand that the Prime Minister was becoming concerned about the constant calls for another referendum from members of his own party and the loss of potential Conservative supporters to the United Kingdom Independence Party (UKIP), but I felt that his speech in January 2013 tended to overemphasise the problems that the EU was facing whilst underplaying the benefits that the UK was deriving from its EU membership. The latter, in my opinion, were considerable, and the creation in 1993 of a fully-functioning single market was, despite its need for further enhancements, a superb achievement. It provided the UK with tariff-free trade to most of Europe, and, effectively, a home market of around 500 million people. Speaking personally, I also enjoyed the ability that EU membership gave UK citizens to travel widely throughout Europe with minimal formalities and without having to worry about customs procedures, particularly when returning to the UK. From enquiries that I had made, I also knew that the EU had many new and important trade deals in its pipeline and that these would over the next few years vastly improve the UK's ability to trade globally on advantageous terms. To put all of this at risk by promising a referendum without, at least, lodging a sensible caveat was, I thought, the height of folly.

By the end of 2015, the Prime Minister had still not made a definite pronouncement about setting a date for a referendum, and I was beginning to wonder whether wiser counsels about holding one had prevailed and the venture had been postponed indefinitely. These hopes were dashed, however, when on 20 February 2016 the Prime Minister announced that a referendum on whether the UK should remain in or leave the EU would be held on 23 June 2016. This decision to go ahead with a referendum without first demanding reasonable safeguards was, I believe, both wrong and irresponsible. To attain the position of prime minister in our great country is a huge honour and privilege, but it also carries with it heavy responsibilities. One of these is, or should be, to do nothing that could potentially cause serious harm to the UK economy and, by extension, to the well-being of the British people. A person is not elevated to the position of prime minister in order that he or she might play Russian roulette with the UK economy. In my view, before agreeing to hold a referendum, the Prime Minister should have thrown down a challenge to those who were demanding a referendum (politicians in his own party and UKIP's Nigel Farage), requiring them to put forward solid evidence –evidence that he could then put to the UK's finest economists and economic organisations for their comments –that leaving the EU would not cause serious damage to the UK's economy. The evidence required could, for example, have consisted of two economic models; one to illustrate the economic effects of leaving the EU and the other to show how the UK economy would progress if we remained. This requirement, I believe, would have been perfectly fair and reasonable, and would, at a stroke, have put David Cameron into a win-win situation. If these leading Brexiteers had risen to the challenge and put forward the required evidence, I am confident that their efforts would have been met by a storm of scorn and derision from most leading economists. On the other hand, if they had refused to meet the challenge but instead continued to fulminate and bluster, then they would, by their own inaction, have exposed themselves as little more than a group of bumptious windbags.

One of the ironies of the situation that the UK found itself in on 20 February 2016 was the fact that during the preceding three years, 2013, 2014 and 2015, the UK economy had been performing well. There were clear signs in 2013 from the UK's Gross Domestic Product (GDP) growth of 2.2 per cent (0.8 per cent more than in 2012 and equivalent to a total increase of £48.4 billion to the UK economy) that the UK had left the austerity mode created by the banking crisis of 2008–2009. This economic progress was emphasised in grand style in 2014 when, with a GDP growth of 2.9 per cent (worth £63.8 billion to the UK economy) the UK had the highest economic growth rate in the EU. In 2015, the GDP growth fell back to 2.4 per cent (a £52.8 billion economic increase); an increase that was, nevertheless, still well above those achieved from 2009 to 2012 and for that matter from 2016 to 2019. It should be noted, too, that the UK's economic growth over the period 2013 to 2015 was considerably higher than the G7 average (the G7 consists of the United States, Japan, Germany, France, UK, Italy and Canada). There was, however, a complete turnaround during the period from 2016 to 2019, when the UK's economic performance was well below the G7 average. This statistical evidence, which is readily obtainable from reputable statistical sources, completely contradicts statements that ministers in the current Brexiteer government were making shortly before the first pandemic lockdown, and I will have more to say about that later.

When David Cameron announced that a referendum would be held on 23 June 2016 to decide whether or not the UK should remain in the EU, I experienced a distinct sense of foreboding. I knew, even if the Prime Minister did not, that the British people had for many years been subjected to a huge amount of anti-EU propaganda in the national press, and that very little had been written that would show the EU in a favourable light. As a result, many people in the UK (including some who were very knowledgeable about most subjects) still knew very little about the EU and its objectives. For example, very few of the people that I had spoken to seemed to have a clear idea of the advantages offered by the single market and what is occasionally referred to as its 'four freedoms', i.e., the unrestricted movement of goods, services, capital and people within the member countries. During the upturn in the UK economy between 2013 and 2015, there had been a substantial increase in the numbers of EU citizens who had come to the UK to take up employment, but this was no more than the 'people' element in the four freedoms was designed to achieve – a ready and speedy response to the increase in available jobs. Many of the people from other EU countries who arrived in the UK during this period were not migrants in the true sense of the word. They were simply people who had come to the UK in order to take advantage of the jobs offered by a burgeoning economy. If for any reason job opportunities dried up, they could either return to their own country or take themselves off to another EU country. If anything that I have written so far suggests that I see the EU through rose-tinted glasses, then I would like to declare that this is definitely not the case. I recognise that as with any large organisation, particularly a truly enormous structure like the EU, there is a constant need for careful scrutiny of policies and procedures to ensure that they become more democratic and do not become overly bureaucratic and authoritarian.

When I stated above that the UK made encouraging economic progress between 2013 and 2015, I was not suggesting that this would have been known and recognised by the public at large. In the more deprived areas of the UK, any signs of an upturn must have been extremely difficult to discern. In August 2014, a study was published which suggested that nine of the ten poorest regions in Northern Europe were in the UK. Northern Europe, for the purposes of the study, consisted of the UK, France, Germany, Belgium, the Netherlands, Denmark, Sweden, Finland, Estonia, Latvia, Lithuania, Austria, Ireland and Luxembourg (Norway, Iceland and the Faroe Islands were excluded because they could not be covered by Eurostat, the statistical office of the European Union). This study, which was carried out by Inequality Briefing and used Eurostat information, found that the poorest region was West Wales, followed by Cornwall, Durham, Lincolnshire, South Yorkshire, Shropshire and Staffordshire, Lancashire, Northern Ireland, Hainaut (Belgium) and East Yorkshire/ North Lincolnshire. At the same time, Inner London was said to be at the top of the ten richest areas in Northern Europe. The study did not, of course, include regions or countries of Southern Europe, e.g., Italy, Spain, Greece and the Balkans, where poorer or equally poor regions could have been found. Nevertheless, the choice of countries to represent Northern Europe offered a very fair comparison. The reason that the UK had so many of the most deprived regions had nothing whatever to do with its being in the EU, and it certainly was not because it was among the poorest of the countries surveyed. It was simply that, for internal reasons that had never been properly addressed by any UK government, inequality in the UK had been allowed to grow to a far greater extent than in any other comparable Northern European country. This was never going to bode well for the referendum on 23 June 2016, as it indicated that many regions of the UK, particularly in England, were likely to be harbouring discontent about their conditions, and likely to express their dissatisfaction by voting against the government.

Chapter 5

The 2016 Referendum

The official campaign period began on 15 April 2016 and ended on polling day, 23 June 2016. It could be characterised as a fight between a remarkably complacent and ill-prepared 'Remain' side, and a 'Leave' side which was relatively well organised and far better prepared for the struggle. From the outset of the campaign, I followed the arguments and studied the tactics very closely, and it soon became apparent to me that the Remainers were in danger of losing a contest which, by any logical or rational reasoning process, they ought to have been able to win by the proverbial mile. Very early on in the campaign, possibly within two or three days of its opening, a prominent Brexiteer (I believe that it was Christopher Grayling, but I am speaking from memory and cannot be absolutely certain) launched on BBC television an astonishing attack on the BBC. He alleged that the BBC was biased against the Leave campaign. This allegation was simply in the form of a 'blanket' statement and did not contain a shred of evidence to support it. This puzzled me at first, as the referendum campaign had only just got under way and the BBC had hardly had time to display bias in any direction. In addition, I was listening to BBC radio and watching BBC television on a daily basis, and could recall nothing that could even remotely be construed as bias.

When I thought a little more about it, the probable reason for the attack seemed fairly obvious. The Leave campaign knew that they held a substantial advantage in the national press, and BBC radio and television were probably the only parts of the media from which they had anything to fear. They were therefore attempting to sideline the BBC or, even better, obtain favourable treatment from the BBC. Either of these outcomes would produce, in varying degrees, an overall media advantage for the Leave campaign. However, new suspicions about what had taken place were aroused by the BBC reaction to the attack, which to me seemed to be abnormal. When a false allegation is made against an organisation or an individual, the normal human reaction is to become highly indignant, and to rebut the accusation in no uncertain terms. Instead, the BBC, without making any admissions of bias, simply stated that they had spoken to their journalists and reminded them of the need to demonstrate impartiality. On the face of it this might seem reasonable, but it appeared clear to me that the journalists involved would have known that the directive had arisen from a Leave campaign complaint and would have taken on board that, if they deviated slightly from the line that they were supposed to take, they had better make sure that it was on the Leave side. There were two aspects of the exchange between the Leave team and the BBC that I was particularly uneasy about. The first of these was the fact that Leave had not provided a vestige of evidence to support their assertion. If their complaint against the BBC was genuine, then I would have expected them to provide at least one example of the bias. The second aspect was the failure of the BBC to ask for evidence. If the Remain side had been sufficiently perceptive at this time, they would have had this entire episode fully investigated immediately to ensure, as far as possible, that nothing untoward had taken place.

I would like to make it clear that I have no real evidence of skulduggery, but have simply given details of the event as I remember it. However, the subsequent BBC coverage of the referendum campaign was appalling. It was littered with inappropriate comparisons of a kind that were referred to at a later date by Kamal Ahmed, then economics director at the BBC, as 'false equivalences', i.e., the BBC were routinely giving as much, sometimes more, prominence to minority views as they were giving to the views of a considerable majority. As an example, I would like to cite a radio broadcast about the opinions of the business community in the UK that I was listening to during the referendum campaign. The BBC broadcaster stated that seventy-five per cent of business people wished the UK to remain in the EU, and this comment was followed by a very short statement. She then continued with a comment that went something like, 'However, twenty-five per cent of business people believe that they would be better off if the UK left the EU', and this announcement was followed by a lengthy interview with one of the twenty-five per cent, which seemed almost interminable. What was the essential truth about this matter that the British public were entitled to know? It was simply that, using the BBC's own statistical information, business people in the UK were strongly, in a ratio of three to one, in favour of the UK's remaining in the EU. Whilst there were no untruths in what the public had been told, the way in which the information had been presented (particularly the protracted interview) amounted to a distortion of the truth in favour of the Leave campaign. There were many similar episodes concerning the BBC's coverage during the referendum campaign, e.g., the occasion when a single Leave-supporting economist's views were put forward as though they were of equal value to those of ten Nobel prize winners who supported Remain!

By the time that the referendum campaign had reached its half-way point, it was obvious to me that Remain were in serious danger of losing the referendum. The exchanges on TV between Remain and Leave politicians were going badly, not because the Leave side were deploying superior arguments but because Leave had found an easy way of avoiding meaningful discussions about the economic consequences of leaving the EU. They simply began to call out 'scaremongering' and 'project fear' whenever Remain tried to instigate an in-depth discussion about the economic consequences of Brexit. Leave were augmenting these defensive soundbites with a very useful attacking one, namely 'take back control' (originally 'take back control of our borders') which they were using as an effective immigration ploy. Although inaccurate (the UK had never taken part in the Schengen Area to which most EU countries belonged which did, to a certain extent, require them to relinquish controls at their borders) the 'take back control' slogan seemed to resonate with many people. Another aspect that seemed to be lost on many members of the public that I spoke to was that the free movement of people element of the 'four freedoms' that the UK had signed up to was a reciprocal measure, i.e., UK citizens were entitled to move to other EU countries for work or retirement purposes and around one million and a half of them had done precisely that. As a person who had worked as an immigration officer in the 1960s when, in theory, the UK had total control of its borders, I knew that the current system had far more benefits for the UK. The average person in the UK, however, could not be expected to be aware of this, and many were likely, therefore, to be misled.

By early June 2016, I felt certain that, unless the Remain side changed tack and started to carry the fight to the Leave side on the immigration issue instead of attempting to run away from it, Remain would lose the referendum. I therefore began to send emails to individuals and organisations that were prominent on the Remain side, imploring them to stop running away from the Immigration issue. Some of these missives went to members of organisations such as 'Stronger in'. Others (in response to emails I had received that bore the names of prominent people such as former Prime Minister Gordon Brown) were addressed to well-known and highly respected politicians (see at Note 1 copies of emails that I sent to Paddy Ashdown and Gordon Brown). Although I doubted whether they would actually be seen by these addressees, I hoped that someone in their teams might be able to give me what I needed; a telephone call in which I could explain my ideas about confronting Leave on immigration. Sadly, the telephone call that I had hoped for never arrived, and there was no perceptible change in Remain's tactics. At the time that I was sending these emails, I, of course, had no idea that any leading Brexiteer would be so careless of the UK's well-being as to take our country out of both the single market and the Customs Union. Nothing as radical and as foolhardy as that had, as far as I was aware, been mooted by the Leave side. If readers look carefully at the content of the emails at Note 1 that I sent to Paddy Ashdown and Gordon Brown, it will be noted that although my forecast that, in the event of Brexit taking place, the French authorities would soon close down the UK border posts in their country, has not yet materialised, two of the main forecasts regarding immigration that I made before the referendum took place have proved correct. One was that a Brexit that banned the free movement of EU people into Britain would preclude any possibility of our obtaining a favourable trade agreement with the EU. This has definitely come to pass, as the trade deal that Boris Johnson signed up to with the EU (about which I shall have more to say later) is causing a huge amount of damage to our economy. The other was that there would be a considerable increase in the numbers of refugees and economic migrants reaching the UK, once what I referred to as the 'EU buffer zone' was removed. This, too, has arrived with a vengeance, as the numbers of such people have, so far, increased ten-fold.

When 23 June 2016 finally arrived and the polling took place, I had no expectation that Remain would be able to win the referendum. The dice, it seemed to me, had been well and truly loaded against them. When the result of the referendum was announced on the following morning, my wife and I, although greatly disappointed, were not surprised. The Leave campaign, although dishonest and deceitful, had successfully engaged with the emotions of many of the voting public. Remain, on the other hand, although far more ready to supply real evidence to support their statements, had not provoked anything like the same emotional response. When considering the efforts of prominent Remain politicians, there were, of course, honourable exceptions. One of these whom I would particularly like to commend was a former prime minister of ours, Sir John Major, who during the campaign wrote an article in favour of Remain that was published in the Daily Telegraph! In this article, Sir John completely dismantled the Leave arguments, and set out succinctly and clearly the many reasons why the UK should remain in the European Union. It was a great pity that his comments were not available at the time to a wider public, as they were full of common-sense observations and insights (see a copy of Sir John Major's article at Note 2).

In my opinion, there were a number of factors that coalesced in a manner that tipped the scale firmly on the side of Leave. I have enumerated, not necessarily in order of importance, some of these below:

1. Despite the fact that the one million plus UK citizens who were residing in other EU countries were obviously going to be seriously affected by a vote to Leave (they would, when Brexit was effected, lose legal rights and privileges in the countries in which they lived), they were not allowed to take part in the 2016 referendum. This, in my opinion, was an outrage against democracy. No UK citizens should have legal rights and privileges removed from them by a Westminster government without their having had any say in the matter.
2. The failure of Remain politicians to confront the Brexiteer politicians directly on the subject of immigration, on the lines

that I suggested earlier. By not challenging their duplicity on this issue and by attempting in interview after interview to change the subject whenever immigration was mentioned, the impression was given that the Remain side had something to hide.

3. The BBC's coverage, on both TV and radio, of the referendum. I have seen suggestions that around two-thirds of British adults watch or listen to BBC programmes, and the way in which these programmes are presented is therefore extremely important. I believe that their frequent insistence on giving minority views on important issues as least as much, sometimes more, prominence as those of the great majority of professionals and experts caused a great deal of confusion in the minds of many members of the public. At a late stage in the campaign the BBC were reporting that many voters were still confused, but the BBC seemed to be oblivious to the fact that they, themselves, were largely responsible for the confusion.

4. The less than wholehearted entry into the fray by Jeremy Corbyn, then Leader of the Labour Party, at a late stage in the proceedings. As a lifelong Labour sympathiser, I find it difficult to understand why he did not engage in the campaign more vigorously and at a much earlier stage. There was plenty of support for Remain in the Labour Parliamentary Party, and many of these MPs would have promoted Remain more energetically if they had been given the right leadership.

All four of the factors that I have mentioned above played their part in the referendum result, and there may well be others that I have not mentioned. However, of the four that I have referred to, I believe that the BBC coverage of the referendum was the most important. I am well aware that, taking circulation figures into account, around 80 per cent of the articles published in our national press about the referendum during the campaign were strongly in favour of Leave, and that that was an important factor in the result. This, however, was only to be expected, as many of our daily newspapers had Brexiteer owners and were bound, therefore, to support Brexit. If a directive has at some time been given by Parliament to the BBC to ensure impartiality, then it would seem likely that it was made, primarily, for party-political events such as general elections, and intended to prevent support being given to a particular political party. However, where referenda which are non-party-political and directly affect the national interest are concerned (the 2016 referendum was a case in point, as most of its principal protagonists belonged to the same political party, i.e., the Conservative Party), then it would not, in my view, be too much to expect the BBC, in addition to reporting what both sides are saying, to seek out and ascertain the truth about the main issues and broadcast it. The BBC, whether it knows it or not or whether it is prepared to recognise it or not, is a national institution and, at such times, should be ready to act in the national interest.

From the comments that I have made above about the BBC, it might be inferred that I have some kind of personal vendetta against the BBC. Nothing, absolutely nothing, could be further from the truth. Among my most cherished childhood memories are the times in the 1930s when I listened to BBC radio programmes in the company of my parents. At the present time the BBC still puts out many interesting and informative programmes on both TV and radio that, if it were not for the Corporation's presence, would probably not be produced. They also employ many highly-talented producers, journalists and broadcasters, and, despite the increased competition, are still making programmes that are among the finest that can be seen or heard today. However, when matters that directly affect the national interest are being debated, such as the momentous decision as to whether the UK should remain in or leave the European Union, the British public are in need of clear, unbiased advice about the claims that are being made. This was not provided during the 2016 referendum campaign, when the BBC simply adopted a lofty position above the fray as though they were umpiring a tennis match. I should like to make it clear that I do not blame the BBC employees for these failings, as they, understandably, could not be expected to jeopardise their careers by exceeding their briefs. Rather, their coverage of the campaign suggested that a malign influence at a high level may exist, or have existed, within the Corporation. Similarly, I do not, in any way, blame the great majority of Leave voters for the damage that has been caused, and is still being caused, to the UK. The Leave side's pronouncements during the referendum campaign were replete with half-truths, distortions and downright lies, and their entire mantra was effectively a huge con; the biggest and most damaging con, in my opinion, that has ever been perpetrated on the British public. Many Leave voters were simply victims of this con, and I, like most people, would never blame the victims of a con for the con.

In the immediate aftermath of the referendum result, I exchanged messages with people who had supported Remain and Remain-supporting organisations, including the Liberal Democrats. In the course of this correspondence, I was asked whether I would consider joining the Liberal Democrats. I replied that, although I had never previously belonged to a political party, I would give this suggestion serious consideration. When I reviewed what had taken place during the referendum campaign, I recognised that the Liberal Democrats, although not as effective as I would have liked them to be, had at least made strenuous efforts to support Remain. This could not be said for either the badly split Conservative Party or a Labour Party which, whilst predominantly Remain-supporting, had an influential minority of Leave supporters. I, therefore, decided to join the Liberal Democrats, and I intend to remain a member of this Party. This was not a difficult decision for me to make as, although I dislike tags such as tory, socialist and lib dem, I had for a very long time regarded myself as a 'left of centre pragmatist' and I am currently living in an area in which only the Liberal Democrats would have a chance of dislodging our Conservative MP. As the final word in the description that I have just made about myself indicates, I have an instinctive dislike of dogma, and when important changes to our economic or social structures are put forward, I expect to see firm evidence to support them. As any perspicacious observer of the 2016 referendum campaign would have noticed, such evidence was totally absent from the Leave side's campaign.

Chapter 6

The Aftermath and the 2019 General Election

Following the success for Leave on 23 June 2016, although I knew that the talks to arrange an orderly departure from the EU and negotiate a satisfactory trade deal would be difficult, I, nevertheless, thought it likely that the UK would be completely out of the EU by 31 December 2018 at the latest. In the event, negotiations proved far more difficult and protracted that anyone had forecast, and three years after the 2016 referendum, the entire Brexit venture was in the balance and, with better leadership in the main opposition parties, might well have been overturned. When David Cameron resigned his position as prime minister about two weeks after the referendum result, the right to succeed him was contested in the Conservative Party and Theresa May emerged the winner. Usually defined in the media, correctly or otherwise, as a Eurosceptic Remainer, Theresa May quickly adopted a strong 'Brexit means Brexit' stance, and gave prominent positions in her new cabinet to three leading Brexiteers, namely David Davis, Boris Johnson and Liam Fox. Presumably to balance these appointments, she also gave several senior government positions to Remainers. She then set about, doggedly and methodically, attempting to implement the referendum result. In order to initiate negotiations on the UK's separation from the EU, she first needed to enable this process by invoking Article 50 of the Lisbon Treaty. Her initial attempt to do this in November 2016 was prevented by the UK's High Court, when it ruled that she needed to obtain the prior approval of Parliament. An appeal against the High Court's ruling was rejected by the Supreme Court in January 2017, and eventually a bill giving her the required approval was passed by the House of Commons in February 2017. Amendments to this bill, tabled by the House of Lords, were rejected by the Commons, and the way was then clear for her to invoke Article 50 in March 2017.

Theresa May then made, from her own and her supporters' points of view, a serious political blunder. In an attempt to bolster her position in Parliament and strengthen her hand in the oncoming negotiations with the EU, she decided in April 2017 to call a snap general election, which would be held in June 2017. Although she started from what appeared to be a strong position in the polls, a series of gaffes and unexpected events and a rather insipid campaign presence combined to erode confidence in her policies. Moreover, her main opponent, Jeremy Corbyn, was surprisingly effective as he campaigned enthusiastically around the UK, and, in contrast to the Prime Minister, appeared to be enjoying the cut and thrust. The outcome of the election, which came as a shock to most of the pundits, was a dangerously reduced majority. In point of fact, had she not been propped up by the Democratic Unionist Party (DUP) (the very people who are, as I am writing this, complaining bitterly about the border in the Irish Sea), she would have been in dire straits. The ten seats that the DUP provided offered her a lifeline, and she decided to soldier on. The three main issues in the separation agreement that she negotiated were the payments that the UK would make to the EU to honour agreements and obligations that the UK had agreed earlier (the so-called divorce bill), the rights of EU nationals who were residing in the UK and the rights of UK citizens who were living in EU countries and a mechanism which would prevent a hard border in Ireland. The first two of these three issues were agreed in a reasonably short period of time, but the Irish border issue was far more difficult and, for a time, seemed virtually intractable.

Before discussing further the eventual results of these negotiations for a separation agreement and their reception in Parliament, I would like to draw attention to information that became available early in 2018, which might reasonably, in my view, have caused Theresa May to pause the entire Brexit process and consider whether, in the light of this new information, the matter should be taken back to the British people. HM Treasury had been instructed (I understand by the Prime Minister) to produce figures to demonstrate the effects on the UK economy of various forms of Brexit. The information provided by HM Treasury showed quite clearly that any form of Brexit would cause considerable damage to the UK economy, and that the differences in the versions assessed were simply matters of degree. For example, the figures provided showed that the 'alternative Chequers scenario', a 'Canada-style free trade agreement' and a 'no-deal Brexit' would lower the UK GDP by, respectively, 3.9 per cent (£85.8 billion), 6.7 per cent (£147.4 billion) and 9.3 per cent (£204.6 billion) annually (see the paper at Note 3 which shows how these monetary calculations were made). This information, predictably, sent leading Brexiteer politicians into paroxysms of rage, and they immediately set about trying to downplay the figures by disputing their accuracy. This was all nonsense, as few people would have claimed that HM Treasury's figures were one hundred per cent accurate or needed to be. They were, however, educated estimates, and it was very noticeable that the Treasury's critics made no attempt to produce figures of their own! Although the Prime Minister was probably unaware of the deficiencies in the organisation and conduct of the 2016 referendum that I have drawn attention to earlier, this new information alone might well have caused Theresa May to rethink her 'Brexit means Brexit' policy. During the 2016 referendum campaign, the British public had not been told by the Leave campaigners that Brexit would be very costly. Indeed, the latter had scoffed at the idea, and dismissed any such forecasts as 'scaremongering' and 'project fear'. However, if, in fact, the Prime Minister did give the matter serious consideration she obviously decided not to pursue this option and continued instead to press on with her Withdrawal Agreement negotiations.

As mentioned earlier, agreements in principle regarding the divorce bill and citizens' rights were reached quite quickly. Understandably, thrashing out the finer details of these issues was more protracted, but this too was accomplished within a reasonable timeframe. Although talks on a comprehensive Free Trade Agreement (FTA) were not due to commence until after the Withdrawal Agreement had been fully agreed and authorised by the respective governing bodies and parliaments on both sides, an outline for a sketchy and non-binding trade deal was also agreed. The main sticking point in the entire process was, as one would have anticipated, the border between Northern Ireland and the Republic of Ireland. Both sides wished to avoid a return to a hard border that would jeopardise the Good Friday Agreement. The two sides, however, put forward radically different proposals for achieving this objective. The EU's proposal was for a 'backstop' which would, effectively, keep Northern Ireland within the Customs Union and the single market until after the FTA had been agreed. This was opposed by the UK, as it would have meant treating Northern Ireland differently from the rest of the UK. Similarly, the UK's suggestion that the whole of the UK should be treated as if it were a 'de facto' part of the EU Customs Union was unacceptable to the EU, primarily because the UK government wanted to retain the right to withdraw unilaterally from the Customs Union at a time of its own choosing. A fudge was eventually agreed in which Michel Barnier, the EU's Chief Negotiator, accepted that the whole of the UK could remain in the Customs Union, provided that the UK in return accepted that it would not be allowed to exit the backstop unless and until the EU agreed that there was no prospect of a return to a hard border. The UK also had to accept special customs arrangements for Northern Ireland and certain level playing field conditions for the whole of the UK.

The Withdrawal Agreement that Theresa May had negotiated with Michel Barnier was disliked by many MPs on both the left and right wings of the political spectrum for totally different reasons. Hard-line Brexiteers and the DUP thought that too many concessions had been made to the EU, whilst the main opposition parties believed that the deal was vastly inferior to the arrangements with the EU that we already had. When the deal was put to Parliament early in 2019, it was voted down on no fewer than three occasions. These setbacks caused Theresa May to resign from her position as PM in late May 2019; a resignation that took effect in June 2019 after Boris Johnson had been selected to succeed her. If she had been successful and had managed to get approval from Parliament for her Withdrawal Agreement, would she have been able to follow that by negotiating a satisfactory Free Trade Agreement? My personal belief is that she would not. By satisfactory, I mean an FTA which mirrored as closely as possible the arrangements that we had in the single market before Brexit, and included the free movement of services and capital as well as goods. In writing this, I am in no way intending to belittle her negotiating skills. She had tried hard and diligently when negotiating the Withdrawal Agreement and had certainly gained the respect of her opposite numbers. The main problem as I see it would have been that in attempting to obtain a favourable FTA for a country that had voluntarily quit the EU and wished to remain aloof from the EU single market and Customs Union, she would, effectively, have been trying to make a silk purse out of a sow's ear. Even if she had managed to make a satisfactory agreement with the EU's main negotiator (an unlikely scenario), any such agreement would almost certainly have been voted down by other EU countries as far too generous to the UK.

When Boris Johnson was chosen by his party to replace Theresa May as prime minister, I recognised that the opposition parties would encounter a formidable and unscrupulous adversary. In his previous journalistic career, although the possessor of a witty turn of phrase, he was not known as a person who would allow the absolute truth to get in the way of a good story. I also felt that his espousal of Leave prior to the 2016 referendum owed as much to the prospects that it would afford him for self-aggrandisement as to a belief in Leave's merits. His attempt to prorogue Parliament in August 2019 (a decision that was condemned as unlawful by the Supreme Court) was a clear indication to me that he would stop at very little to achieve his objectives. Fortunately for Boris Johnson, the main opposition leader, Jeremy Corbyn, failed to recognise that by the spring of 2019 a pronounced change had taken place in the public perception of Brexit. I am confident that if he had overseen a change of policy in the Labour Party regarding Brexit by June 2019, and had adopted a firm 'End Brexit and revoke Article 50' policy, and (this is crucial) with the assistance of his Remainer MPs had backed this up with a massive nationwide campaign, he would have picked up a huge amount of additional support for this new policy. Plenty of new information had emerged by early 2019 to confirm that Brexit would be seriously damaging to the UK; in addition to the HM Treasury forecasts mentioned earlier, the prestigious merchant bank, Goldman Sachs, stated in January 2019 that the uncertainty created by the Brexit vote had since June 2016 been costing the UK £600 million per week (£31.2 billion per year). At around the same time, another merchant bank (the name of which I did not record) made a similar estimate about the same matter. These statements indicated that the mere threat of Brexit had been causing a considerable loss to the UK's GDP.

Readers might wonder why I was so confident that there had been a significant change in the public mood about Brexit. I was not, of course, suggesting that a large proportion of those who had voted for Brexit had, by the summer of 2019, changed their minds. However, it should be recognised that if just ten per cent of those who had supported Brexit in 2016 had changed their minds or were having serious doubts about the claims that had been made for Brexit, that would have been enough to overcome the Brexit vote in a further referendum. During the summer of 2019, I helped out on several occasions in public on Liberal Democrat or Dorset for Europe stalls and was astounded to see in the grass polls that were conducted (members of the public were invited to indicate on a large paper sheet their preferences for various forms of Brexit and for End Brexit) that the public were consistently casting more votes for End Brexit than for all the Brexit versions added together. Dorset at the time of the 2016 referendum was a strongly Eurosceptic county, and every voting district had, without exception, voted for Leave. I thought it reasonable to suppose, therefore, that if there had been a change of mood in Dorset, this was likely to be mirrored in many other regions of the UK. In Parliament, Boris Johnson's position was looking increasingly precarious, as his slender advantage in MPs was being slowly whittled away. During the autumn of 2019, John Bercow was performing heroics in the Speaker's Chair as, time and again, he managed to foil Boris Johnson's machinations (much to the annoyance of the Brexiteer press, whose attacks on the Speaker were becoming increasingly hysterical). At this point, I thought that the tide had really turned in favour of Remain, and that there was a good chance that we would be able to hold a third (not second, because we had already had two referendums on the same subject in 1975 and 2016) and final referendum in the near future.

Unfortunately for the UK, at around the end of October 2019, two political parties, the Liberal Democrats and the Scottish National Party (SNP), allowed themselves to be goaded by Boris Johnson into accepting his ideas for an early general election. One would have thought that the mere fact that Boris Johnson had been pushing the need for a general election should have made them extremely wary. Labour, it seems, felt that in these circumstances they had no choice but to give their assent for a general election, and smaller anti-Brexit parties followed suit. Boris Johnson, who probably could scarcely believe his good fortune, lost no time in taking advantage of the situation and speedily arranged for a general election to be held on 12 December 2019. In this way, the forces for Remain, in what can only be described as a moment's madness, threw away all the good work that had been accomplished in Parliament during the previous few months. The Remain parties could, and should, have held out for another referendum, and it seems likely to me that Boris Johnson, with his lack of a parliamentary majority, would have had to give way eventually. In a referendum every vote would count, whereas in a general election, with our current electoral system, there was always the danger that tribalism would prevail and that many votes would be wasted. Why precisely the Liberal Democrat leader, Jo Swinson, agreed to the holding of a general election is a difficult question to answer. She was clearly disappointed with Labour's reluctance to line up with the other 'Stop Brexit' parties, and this may have inclined her, wrongly I would say, to treat Labour as a Brexit party. Whatever the truth might be, there can be no doubt that Jo's decision to agree, in the company of the SNP and other parties, to a general election was a catastrophic error of judgement.

When the campaigning for the 2019 general election began, vicious and sustained attacks on the Labour leader, Jeremy Corbyn, soon got under way in the Brexiteer press. Although these attacks were undoubtedly damaging, I believe that the main reason for the failure of his general election campaign was the fact that he had not embraced fully an unequivocal 'End Brexit' stance several months earlier. If he had done this, he and other Labour politicians would have been able to pursue this policy vigorously on TV and radio during the election campaign. In particular, it would have greatly assisted him during his head-to-head confrontations with Boris Johnson on TV. Rather than trying to adopt a neutral position on Brexit, which pleased very few people and alienated many, he would have been able to carry the fight to a rather, in my opinion, unconvincing Boris Johnson far more effectively. Instead, to people who were heartily sick of hearing about Brexit, his proposal to spend a further period of at least six months while he negotiated yet another withdrawal agreement and then hold a third referendum must have sounded like an eternity. If Jeremy Corbyn had adopted an 'End Brexit' stance about six months before the 2019 general election he could easily have monitored opinion polls and, in the unlikely event of their not having been influenced favourably by his initiative, could have held firm for a referendum rather than an election. Remaining in the EU, with full access to the single market and the EU's burgeoning trade deals, would have provided his general election manifesto with a firm and reliable economic base. There wasn't, in my opinion, a great deal wrong with his manifesto, except that he was planning to do too much too soon and, as one commentator put it, people couldn't see the wood for the trees.

Regardless of whether Labour endorsed scrapping Brexit or not, it was imperative for Labour, the Liberal Democrats and the Greens to co-operate fully. The Liberal Democrats should have withdrawn candidates from all Labour-held seats, and pressured other Remain parties to take similar action. Labour, in return, should have removed their candidates from any seats held by the Liberal Democrats and other Remain parties. Remain's representation in marginal Conservative-held seats should have been decided by mutual consent, with the principle of one Remain candidate per seat being adhered to wherever possible. At this momentous occasion in our history, the national interest should have been paramount. Regretfully, the much-needed alliance of Remain parties did not materialise, and when 12 December 2019 arrived and the votes were cast, our archaic electoral system, as Boris Johnson had correctly calculated, gave the supporters of Brexit a stunning victory and an overall majority of around 80 seats.

The result of the 2019 general election has since been trumpeted in the Brexiteer press and in other parts of the media as a clear indication that the voting public wanted to 'get Brexit done'. Even the Labour Shadow Chancellor at the time, John McDonnell, made a comment which supported this idea. Actually, when one looks closely at the votes cast for each of the many parties that participated, far more people voted for parties that supported having a further referendum than for parties that wanted Brexit. Some time ago, I read an article which said that Professor Sir John Curtice of Strathclyde University had examined the voting figures and found that fifty-three per cent of the voters who had participated had voted for parties that wanted a further referendum. As this information had been obtained at second hand, I decided to have a close look at the voting figures myself, and I found that fifty-three per cent of the participants had indeed voted for parties that wanted a further referendum, forty-six per cent had voted for parties that supported Brexit and one per cent voted for parties that gave no clear indication of their wishes. The voting figures for the 2019 general election did not, therefore, support in any way the idea that the result was a clear endorsement of Brexit. Rather, they had corresponded very closely to the figures that I had seen when, as I mentioned earlier, I had helped on pro EU stalls in Dorset during summer 2019. This begs the question, 'Could Jeremy Corbyn have won the general election on 12 December 2019?'. I firmly believe that, provided that he had adopted an 'End Brexit' policy by June 2019 and, as I suggested earlier, had backed it up with a nationwide information campaign about the effects of Brexit on the UK economy and the well-being of the British people, he could have led Labour to victory. To what extent this error of judgement arose from bad advice is difficult to say, but it seems likely that it played a part.

Chapter 7

Brexit and the Economy

In this chapter and the two that follow, I shall be writing about three of the main issues that were prominent during the referendum campaign, the economy, immigration, and freedom and sovereignty, and commenting about the effects that Brexit has since had upon them. I make no apologies for starting with the economy, as this was by far the most important of these three issues. Without a strong and buoyant economy that is performing to the best of its ability, it will be difficult to fund our essential public services adequately, to tackle climate change effectively and to put in hand the actions needed to improve standards of living in our more deprived regions. At the present time our current prime minister, Boris Johnson, is talking a great deal about 'levelling up', but if the finances are not available to support this action such promises are little more than empty words.

I should like to deal first with the period from 23 June 2016 until the end of 2019, when the UK was neither fully in nor out of the EU and effectively in a state of limbo. Although the country was able to trade relatively normally, I have seen figures that indicated that the UK's exports to the EU dropped by about five per cent during this period. There was also, understandably in view of the UK's expressed intention to leave, a reluctance in EU countries to establish new contacts with UK companies. Another worrying, although eminently predictable, consequence of the 2016 referendum vote was the need that overseas-owned UK manufacturers felt to relocate to other EU countries. A number of important manufacturers, including the Japanese car company, Honda, have relocated either to other EU countries or to their own countries. In addition, at least one prominent UK manufacturer moved its production during this period from the UK to an Asian country. The value of the pound sterling dropped appreciably immediately after the referendum result, and, as I mentioned in an earlier chapter, economic growth showed a considerable fall during the period from mid-2016 to the end of 2019. Some banks and financial institutions attempted to estimate the financial losses suffered by the UK during this period. In early 2019, Goldman Sachs estimated that the UK had been losing £600 million per week (£31.2 billion a year) since the 2016 vote. A few months later in about July, the then head of the Bank of England, Mark Carney, estimated that the UK was then losing two per cent of GDP (the total UK economy), which, according to figures given by Rishi Sunak in 2020 (see Note 3 of Endnotes) equated to an annual loss of £44 billion. In 2018, HM Treasury, at the government's behest, made estimates for the 'chequers' version of Brexit and for a 'no deal' Brexit, and these suggested that by the 2030s the UK would be losing annually from around £85.8 billion (for the Chequers deal) to a blood-curdling £204.6 billion (for 'no deal').

Probably, the best estimate of total losses from 23 June 2016 to 31 December 2019 was the one made in January 2020 by Bloomberg Economics (part of the huge Bloomberg organisation), which was £130 billion. The date that this was published is important, as the general election had been held in the previous month, December 2019, and they clearly were not electioneering or attempting to influence an election.

The Bloomberg European Headquarters, built between 2010 and 2017 in the heart of the City of London, cost £1 billion to build, and currently houses around 4,000 employees. If any organisation has the facilities, the personnel and the expertise to make a reliable estimate of the Brexit losses, this one certainly does. Moreover, Bloomberg also forecast that Brexit would cost the UK a further £70 billion during 2020, thus causing a total loss between 23 June 2016 and 31 December 2020 of around £200 billion! These losses, of course, referred only to losses before the end of 2020, and excluded any ongoing losses that would occur after Brexit was finally completed.

The fact is that no European country, even one as relatively wealthy as the UK, can afford to throw away revenue on this gigantic scale, and still expect to have top-notch public services. No leading Brexiteer has ever acknowledged these huge losses publicly, and this is only to be expected as any acknowledgment would show Brexit in a very bad light. Indeed, on Question Time programmes on BBC TV shortly before the 2020 lockdown, Brexiteer ministers on the panels were still claiming that the UK had been in austerity mode for the last ten years, and that this had been caused by the Labour government's reactions to the international banking crisis of 2008–2009. The UK had, they insisted, enjoyed ten years of 'good economic management' during the period 2011-2020. Ludicrous though these statements were (probably, at this time, the latest diktats from Dominic Cummings), they went completely unchallenged by both panels and audiences. It would have been interesting if one of the ministers had been asked to explain how squandering £130 billion up to 31 December 2019 and getting nothing in return but a poorer country with run-down public services and an uncertain future could be equated with good economic management, but nobody (not even the Labour Shadow Chancellor who was sitting on one of the panels) put that question. I can only presume that she was, at this time, under strict instructions from her party leader, Sir Keir Starmer, not, under any circumstances, to mention the word 'Brexit'. Similarly, the Brexiteer politicians could also have been asked to explain how the UK had managed to have the highest economic growth rate in the EU in 2014 when it was, allegedly, suffering from a sustained period of austerity at that time. This type of Brexiteer lie can easily be disproved by looking at the UK's GDP year-on-year growth figures for the decade 2011 to 2020 (readily obtainable from the Office for National Statistics). Just bear in mind that the loss of only one per cent of GDP equates to a loss of £22 billion. During the years 2018 and 2019 (before the arrival of Covid-19) the UK's GDP growth rates dropped to levels that had not been seen since 2011 and 2012. Other countries in the EU and the G7 were experiencing an upturn in their economies in 2018 and 2019, and it is abundantly clear from this that the UK's loss of economic growth during the same period can only have been caused by the vote for Brexit.

Encouraged by his success in the December 2019 general election, Boris Johnson lost no time in packing his Conservative government with Brexiteers, and in pressing on with his negotiations with the EU for a Free Trade Agreement. The negotiations that took place in 2020 between the EU and the UK were lengthy and fractious. Boris Johnson insisted that the UK should leave both the EU single market and the Customs Union, and this effectively precluded any possibility of the UK's getting a good trade deal with the EU. The Northern Ireland border problem was for a long time looking insoluble, until Boris Johnson took over from his chief negotiator and made concessions to the EU that, in all probability and in the longer term, he had no intention of keeping. One of these concessions, contrary to what he had promised previously, ensured that there would indeed be a border in the Irish Sea. The net result of all of this was an FTA which was significantly worse than the trade agreement that the UK had enjoyed as an EU member. The talks had probably been the first bilateral trade negotiations in history where the two participants were endeavouring to take themselves further away from each other, rather than closer together. Although the Northern Ireland border problem had dominated the talks, the agreed FTA was obviously certain to cause significant disruption to normal trade (goods, services and capital) between the UK and the EU. I doubt that many people in the UK realised just how important the single market had been in the provision of so many essential items to the UK and to our supply chains. Everything had been working like a well-oiled machine, and it was as easy to send a parcel from London to Helsinki as from London to Harrogate. The verdict of most UK economists on the overall effect of the FTA was an annual loss of five per cent of GDP (around £110 billion according to figures provided by Rishi Sunak). The only dissent that I heard came from arch-Brexiteer, Liam Fox, who, when interviewed by the BBC, predictably said that loss figures could not be estimated as there were 'too many variables'. In fact, precise figures of annual losses were not absolutely necessary, as all that the public needed to know was that it would be a huge amount of money.

When the Brexiteer government's trade agreement with the EU came into effect in January 2021, many of the worst predictions were confirmed in the first few months. Many small businesses that had previously been exporting successfully to EU countries went bust, having been unable to cope with the increased tariffs placed upon their products and the deluge of additional paperwork that had descended upon them. For example, a thriving shellfish industry, which naturally depended upon being able to move its products to their intended markets without delay, sustained severe damage. Inward investment into the UK, which had already been severely reduced during the UK's four and a half years' limbo period, virtually dried up. Our exports of both goods and services to EU countries had declined appreciably, and our current account deficit was increasing. Sterling appeared to be weakening, and was seemingly becoming dangerously isolated. As I write at this moment (in the middle of 2022), the one part of the UK that is doing relatively well economically is Northern Ireland, which, uniquely, is still able to trade as if it had remained in the single market. For the greater part of the UK, the overseas trade prospects are looking increasingly dire. Before the UK entered the EU on 1 January 1973, the UK was frequently being referred to as 'The Sick Man of Europe'. Even though, at that period, the single market had not been fully established, the UK's economic growth rate had for many years been lagging behind the growth rate that had been enjoyed by the then six member states. It had been recognised by successive UK governments that the UK was in need of a much larger home market, and that was a major reason behind the UK's entry into the EU. This market had later expanded into a home market of over 500 million people when, almost incomprehensibly, our voters were persuaded to abandon it. One does not need to be an Einstein to recognise that a tariff-free and bureaucracy-free market of 500 million people is far more attractive, both to our own exporters and to overseas investors into the UK, than an internal market of around 68 million people. Moreover, where international trade is concerned, geographical proximity is extremely important; a point that was emphasised in March 2019 in an article by a former prime minister of Australia, Kevin Rudd (see a copy of this article at Note 4). If Kevin Rudd, speaking from some distance away, could see so clearly where the true interests of the UK lay, it was surprising that so many UK politicians were unable to do this.

Brexiteer politicians frequently talk about the 'wonderful' new opportunities provided by Brexit for increased trade with countries outside the EU, and the fact that we can now make our own trade agreements. This, in my opinion, is complete and utter drivel. It is very noticeable that Brexiteer politicians repeat this statement about new trade opportunities practically word for word, but never attempt to spell out precisely what these new opportunities are. When I last checked the available information about EU trade agreements in early July 2022, I learned that the EU had to that date made, on behalf of its member countries, 107 Free Trade Agreements with countries outside the EU. In addition, 9 more were in course of negotiation, and a further 25 were on hold. The 107 FTAs include economic giants like Japan (the world's third largest economy) and countries that are important to the UK like Canada and, very recently, New Zealand. The EU's FTA with New Zealand, for which negotiations were started in 2018, was concluded less than two weeks ago. Negotiations for an FTA with Australia, which also began in 2018, are, as far as I am aware, still ongoing. The simple fact is that if the UK were still a member of the EU, our country would today be enjoying on advantageous terms unprecedented access to global markets. It is true that many countries that have made trade agreements with the EU have agreed to roll over their EU deals so that they can continue to benefit the UK. However, the great majority of trade agreements that the UK currently has with overseas countries are EU rollovers, and not new trade deals that the UK has negotiated since Brexit (as some Brexiteers would like the British public to believe). I have no claim to be an economist, but I do know that where bilateral trade negotiations are concerned the side that has the most economic power usually holds the advantage. There is no country or trading bloc in the world at the present time that has more economic clout than the EU. With (when the UK was a member) three of its constituent countries in the world's top ten economies and many other, by world standards, substantial economies, the suggestion by Brexiteers that the UK, acting alone, could make better trade deals than the EU used to make on its behalf has always seemed absurd to me. Even if the UK was able to make a comprehensive agreement with the relatively new economic bloc known as the Comprehensive and Progressive Agreement for Trans-Pacific Partnership (CPTPP) – a bloc which currently comprises eleven countries including Japan, Canada, Australia and New Zealand as well as some Central and South American countries – it would not come close to compensating for the loss of trade in goods, services and capital with the EU's single market that has occurred, and will continue to occur, through Brexit.

Possibly, when one studies carefully the economic benefits of remaining in or leaving the EU, the most telling factor was the reluctance of leading Brexiteers, both during the 2016 referendum campaign and subsequently, to put forward economic models in support of whatever version of Brexit they were advocating. The no-deal Brexit, in particular, when one thinks carefully about what its proponents were suggesting, screamed out for supporting evidence. They were proposing that the UK should abandon an economic system which we knew, or ought to have known, worked perfectly well, in favour of one that was not only untried and untested but would, according to the Treasury and other forecasters, be horrendously expensive. The finance needed to produce economic models has never been a problem for the leading Brexiteers, as they are either wealthy themselves or have wealthy backers. The only logical conclusion, therefore, was that they were aware that any model that they might have produced would have been rubbished to such an extent by the UK's leading economists that it would have completely destroyed what little economic credibility they had.

Chapter 8

Brexit and Immigration

It was widely reported that deprivation and lack of hope in some areas of the UK played a significant part in the successful Leave vote, and, as the most deprived parts of the UK generally supported Leave, there is obviously much truth in this. This did not explain, however, why many people in relatively affluent areas decided to vote for Leave. The constituency in which I lived at the time of the 2016 referendum, Runnymede, and its neighbouring constituency of Woking where many of my friends resided, could not, by any stretch of imagination, be described as deprived, and yet both areas (Runnymede in particular) had sizeable numbers of Leave voters. Runnymede, in fact, voted for Leave and Woking narrowly voted for Remain. During the referendum campaign I interviewed about a dozen people (mostly at my local golf club) and was astounded to find that more than a half of them were expecting to vote for Leave. When I probed their opinions further the reason became blindingly obvious –their main, and sometimes only, concern was immigration. Some were afraid that the UK would be invaded by eighty million Turks (one of the more ridiculous Brexiteer claims) if the UK remained in the EU. Others were impressed by the 'take back control' soundbite that was being repeated ad nauseam by

Brexiteers in TV programmes and on the radio. Therefore, being unaware of the extent to which the UK's trading economy was reliant upon access to the EU's single market and its trade agreements, and of the many important co-operative ventures that the UK had with the EU, e.g., co-operation in scientific research, cultural activities and numerous matters involving national security, they had decided that Leave would be the best option.

As I mentioned in an earlier chapter, I made strenuous efforts during the 2016 referendum campaign to persuade the Remain side to stop running away from immigration and to start carrying the fight to the Leave side on the immigration issue. As an antidote to 'take back control', I wanted Remain to put forward energetically the point that placing immigration controls on EU citizens would preclude any possibility of the UK's getting a favourable trade agreement with the EU. Similarly, I wanted Remain to emphasise that EU citizens working in the UK, far from being the spongers that some parts of the Brexiteer media were suggesting, were actually making a considerable contribution to the UK economy (£4.7 billion net according to the last annual statistic that I have seen). I also wanted Remain to explain that the position regarding refugees and economic migrants from outside the EU would, in the event of a successful vote for Brexit, become much more serious. There were unprecedented numbers of these unfortunate people around the world, particularly in parts of Africa and Asia, and many would welcome an opportunity to get to the UK, where they could claim asylum. Around a million and a half such people, primarily Syrian refugees but also migrants from Africa, were believed to have entered the EU via Italy and Greece during the eighteen months prior to the 2016 June referendum. The UK had been largely insulated from this huge influx, partly through the generosity of fellow EU countries but also because the southern EU countries had, effectively, been acting as a buffer zone. This zone, I wanted Remain to tell the public, would disappear if we left the EU, and immigrants arriving in Southern Europe would simply be fast-tracked through to the UK. We would then find refugees and migrants arriving on our doorstep in numbers that we would be unable to cope with. Both fears have since been fully realised, and anyone who believes that the tenfold increase since Brexit in the number of people arriving on our beaches in rubber boats is purely coincidental either hasn't thought the matter through properly or is extremely naïve. Relations between countries are not entirely dissimilar to relations between individuals. If a person turns his back upon his friends, the likelihood is that his friends will turn their backs upon him. When a country acts in a similar manner to friendly countries, the affected countries are hardly likely to be sympathetic towards the offending country's immigration requirements. The current proposal to deport illegal entrants to a remote African country, Rwanda, (which is certain to provoke worldwide condemnation if put into effect) is a classic example of how a government, having caused a minor immigration problem to become a major one, can resort to an arbitrary and, possibly, illegal act in an attempt to remedy a situation which they themselves created. We are in need of good friends around the world, particularly amongst our nearest neighbours; not people who are hostile or at best indifferent.

It might come as a surprise to some people, but the UK does have an ongoing need for useful workers. With an ageing population and people in general spending smaller proportions of their lives in employment, additional workers are required to help provide for the increasing numbers of citizens who are receiving higher education or living into advanced old age. I, for example, have now spent less than one half of my life in full-time employment. My father, in contrast, spent well over two-thirds of his life fully employed. During the long period of 48 years that the UK passed as a full member of the EU, the UK, right across its employment spectrum, benefited greatly from workers from the other

EU countries. At the higher levels, well-qualified people were able to take on important roles in many areas such as, for example, the NHS and banking. These people represented a real bargain, as the UK did not have to pay for their education or maintain them while they were students. Many of our EU employees were simply transient workers performing tasks in our seasonal and hotel industries. They were extremely useful in helping the UK to build up a sizeable tourist industry. Even at what might be regarded as the lower levels, EU people were willing to do, and carry out well, work that British people in general did not wish to undertake, e.g., fruit-picking. As far as longer-term employees are concerned, the contributions of EU people who worked in care homes all over our country should not be overlooked.

Among the large numbers of EU visitors that we used to get annually were around one million teenagers who, sometimes staying with British families, came here to learn English. I have read reports that suggest that the greater part of this huge annual influx, which usually involved relatively short stays in the UK, has now ceased. This, in my opinion, was another 'own goal' for the UK, as it was very desirable that these youngsters should come to our country, not only to learn English and support the small industry that arranged their learning programmes and accommodation, but also, hopefully, to give them a good experience of life in our country. It needed to be realised that a small proportion of these young people would, in due course, go on to obtain prominent positions, e.g., in politics or business, in their own countries, and a friendly disposition towards the UK would certainly have been to our benefit. One outcome that was greatly assisted by our EU membership was the pre-eminence of the English language. I was extremely proud of the way that English had advanced to become the world's leading language, and the lingua franca of the EU. This advance has now been put into jeopardy, not immediately of course, but certainly in the future. Too much has been talked about the movement of EU nationals into the UK, and very little has been said about the ability that freedom of movement gave UK citizens to move in the opposite direction. As I remarked in an earlier chapter, it was diabolical that UK citizens living in other EU countries were not permitted to take part in the 2016 referendum.

The idea that our needs for additional workers could be covered adequately by a work permit system is totally misconceived. As I realised when I was working as an Immigration Officer many years ago, the introduction of a large slice of bureaucracy immediately creates a considerable roadblock for UK businesses when they have an urgent need to recruit employees. Quite often, it can take a considerable time for an application to be approved when an official, sitting in a remote office, is trying to decide whether or not the applicant ticks all the right boxes. In most cases, there is no substitute for direct recruitment by employers, who can see the applicant before them and make a timely decision as to whether or not he or she can join their workforce. Another factor that should be taken into account is that there are many countries within the EU that regularly provide employment to workers from other parts of the EU. These workers have no need to obtain work permits, so why should they wish to apply for a work permit before coming to the UK for work and then, for example, have to worry about permit expiry dates, when they have no such problems in other EU countries. In response to complaints about labour shortages in the UK since January 2021, our Brexiteer government has made attempts to attract the required EU workers with special work permit schemes, but the take-up of these invitations has so far been derisory. It would, of course, be possible, via the normal work permit procedures and after the expenditure of a great deal of time and effort, to recruit some of the required workers, e.g., for the NHS, from countries outside the EU. This action, which is already taking place to a certain extent, would certainly help the current situation but would not be without its drawbacks. Such workers would probably be more inclined to want to remain permanently in the UK, and their recruitment would seem to defeat the main objective of those who supported Leave at the ballot box, i.e., less immigration.

When the UK was a full member of the EU, there was a tendency among British politicians, even among those who were definitely pro-EU, to regard the 'people' element in the single market's four freedoms as something that the UK had to put up with in order to obtain the other three, i.e. the free movement of goods, services and capital, and I must admit that I did, for a while, see this matter in a similar light. However, the more that I have observed how the 'people' part of the four freedoms worked in practice, the more I have come to realise that this element, far from being an appendage, was actually an essential part of the four freedoms. The unprecedented numbers of job vacancies in the UK that have been reported in recent months, which must have applied a brake to our economic recovery following the pandemic, would not have arisen to anything like the same extent if EU labour had continued to be readily available.

Chapter 9

Freedom and Sovereignty

Without genuine freedoms, sovereignty, in my opinion, is totally worthless. One of the most sovereign countries in the world today is North Korea: it pays little or no attention to anything that the United Nations or any other international organisation has to tell it, and seemingly does not take a great deal of notice of its main backer, China. Its sovereignty is just about as complete as any country's could be in the modern world, but how many people in the UK would want to live there? I would guarantee that very few would, and so I will first concentrate on freedom. On 1 March 2018, I was watching a BBC Question Time programme when a lady in the audience, who appeared to be about sixty years of age, announced that people in the UK under the age of forty-five did not know what it was like to live in a free country. A quick mental calculation told me that we had been in the EU for exactly forty-five years and two months; hence the reason for her choice of age. My initial reaction was to wonder what kind of ivory tower she had lived in prior to the UK's entry into the EU. I then realised that I, by a remarkable coincidence, was exactly ninety years and four months old at that point in time, and that I had spent exactly one half (the first half) of my life simply as a UK citizen and the second half as a UK citizen within the EU. In which half had I experienced the most genuine freedom? Well, I knew with absolute certainty that it was not the first half, and I was confident that many people of my generation, particularly those who like myself had grown up in an inner city, would have had a similar experience.

During the 1930s when, as I mentioned in an earlier chapter, I was the youngest member of a small but politically aware family in east-central London, I was encouraged to listen in to and even to ask questions about political discussions that my father had regularly with close relatives and friends. I soon came to realise that I had uncles who were experiencing the great freedom of being unemployed for long periods despite strenuous efforts to find work, and I became painfully aware of how difficult life was for many people. Class distinctions, I learned, were rampant, and seemingly permeated through just about every stratum of society. Discipline, generally, in London schools was draconian, and one school that I attended, thankfully for quite a short period, was more like a torture chamber than a place of learning. At about the age of eight years, I did acquire a certain classroom prestige through being the only member of my class to have been abroad. My classmates had never been out of the UK, and some had never even been out of London! What did my going abroad amount to? It was a day trip to Calais. Returning to the lady who believed in 2018 that people under the age of forty-five did not know what it was like to live in a free country, it beggars belief that anyone could imagine that people living, say, in the 1930s and 1940s were experiencing more genuine freedoms than people living in the 1990s and 2000s. By genuine freedoms, I mean, to give a few examples, the ability to exercise free speech, to have regular and meaningful employment, to have educational opportunities which were far superior to those that had existed during most of our pre-EU period, to be able to travel widely to neighbouring countries without bureaucratic interference, to be able to enjoy clean beaches and unpolluted rivers and, above all, during the time that we were in the EU, to enjoy a peaceful and co-operative existence for forty-eight years with our fellow EU countries. Some improvements whilst we were in the EU such as easier and cheaper air travel would probably have developed anyway if we had remained outside, but others would not. Too many vested interests would have been in the way, and, since we left, there have already been unpleasant signs that some UK businesses believe that, by the act of removing ourselves from the EU, they have been given carte blanche to start polluting our rivers and coastal areas again.

During the 1930s and 1940s, six-day working weeks were the norm for most employees in the UK. When I started work in December 1941, Saturday was a full working day, and, as far as I can recall, this continued to be the case until I joined the Admiralty in late 1950. Moreover, in the 1930s and the first half of the 1940s, paid annual leave for employees was the exception rather than the rule. Before WW2, my father received one week's unpaid annual leave from his GWR employer. The only real perk that he received from his employer was free train travel for himself and his family when he was on his one week's holiday. This did enable us to take our annual holiday in places like Blackpool and Paignton, as well as the usual Kentish resorts, such as Ramsgate and Margate. This was considerably more than most working families could do, as they were largely restricted to resorts that were reasonably close to where they lived. It took a long time for trade unions in our country to understand that, far from representing a threat to trade unionists, the EU offered the best prospects for all kinds of employee rights. Sadly, one head of a large UK union does not seem to have got the message, and is still trying to inflict his anti-EU beliefs upon the Labour Party.

When health considerations are taken into account, the work that the EU did in devising and insisting upon better food labelling should be given the credit that it deserved. This, far from being an unwelcome piece of bureaucracy that was imposed upon us, has had real and tangible health benefits for the entire nation. As more and more information about the effects of nutrition upon our health becomes available, the value that we get from being able to see at a glance whether a product contains, for example, too much fat or too much sugar, is priceless. Another freedom that the UK has lost since it left the EU is the Erasmus scheme, which enabled our young people to live, study and work abroad, usually during gap years in their own studies. This EU scheme was well funded, and it offered our students valuable additional studies and work experience abroad. A younger relative of my wife, whilst undertaking studies for the legal profession in the UK, was able to spend a gap year studying in Strasbourg, France. After gaining her legal qualifications, she was able to carry out further studies for one year in Florence, Italy, and she later carried out legal work in Madrid. Our Brexiteer government turned down an option, given to them by the EU, to retain Erasmus, and instead produced their own Turing scheme. Doubts persist, however, as to whether or not the Turing scheme will be adequately funded (presuming, of course, that the Turing scheme does actually get off the ground and was not just another Boris Johnson knee-jerk reaction). Other losses that the UK has sustained, although not freedoms in the conventional sense, are access to the EU's Structural and Investment Funds and its Rural Development Fund. These are losses that will undoubtedly have an impact in our more deprived regions.

Turning to sovereignty, this is a concept which, for countries like the UK when it was still in the EU, seemed to me to have a somewhat nebulous quality. During our long period as a member of the EU, I cannot think of anything that seriously jeopardised our ability to govern ourselves effectively, or interfered with our normal State activities. In all important matters, we were, as far as I could see, in full control of our own destiny. We organised our own elections and elected our own governments (albeit with an archaic electoral system which is still not as democratic as it should be), and decided our own defence alliances. It seems fairly obvious that there would be complete chaos if all twenty-seven member countries (twenty-eight when the UK was a member) in the EU were allowed to go their own way in matters like, for example, food hygiene, labelling and medicines. Common standards right across the EU were essential, and so, therefore, was the need for a European Court of Justice which could adjudicate on any problems that might arise.

When the UK was an EU member, our country was, in common with the other twenty-seven members, required to pool a small proportion of its sovereignty in order to ensure that economic and social procedures remained in line. The need for the UK to have to do this, and to adjust our national laws accordingly, was blown up out of all proportion by the Brexiteer press which routinely presented it as a serious infringement of our sovereignty. In fact, the relatively small amount of sovereignty that the UK ceded was a small price to pay for the economic benefits and increased national prestige that EU membership provided. If, after the UK left the EU, we had not been able to obtain as rollovers so many of the EU's trade agreements with other countries, we would have been obliged to trade globally under World Trade Organization (WTO) rules to a much greater extent. In doing this, the UK would have had no choice but to follow a raft of WTO regulations. It is understandable that countries that obtained independence in the twentieth century after having been exploited by colonial masters for many years should be concerned about losing sovereignty. However, developed countries, particularly those that trade extensively on a global scale, should be mature enough to understand that co-operation between countries is essential in the modern world. If doing this requires the pooling of a small amount of sovereignty, then that, in my opinion, is of no great consequence.

Chapter 10

Covid-19 and Brexit

Nothing could pinpoint the sheer monumental folly of Brexit more clearly than Covid-19, which has been ravaging the UK since it first made its appearance here in early 2020. This may sound like an exaggerated, or even improbable, declaration, bearing in mind that the two items involved, Covid-19 and Brexit, obviously have no direct connection. Covid-19 would have arrived in the UK regardless of whether or not Brexit had preceded it, and would still, in either case, have caused heavy casualties. In what way, therefore, did the vote in favour of Brexit make a difference? It is simply that without Brexit, it is likely that Covid-19 would have encountered a UK whose vital public services had not been decimated during the three and a half years immediately prior to its arrival, and, in particular, would have found an NHS that was much better prepared and equipped for the challenge.

Very few people that I have spoken to have heard of Exercise Cygnus, and I must confess that I had been unaware of it until it was brought to my attention in April 2020. I then found that a considerable amount of information about it had been published on 29 March 2020 in an extensive article in the Sunday Telegraph. The two journalists who produced the article appeared to have interviewed a large number of politicians, government employees, academics and senior NHS officials (both administrators and medically qualified persons) and, although the existence of Exercise Cygnus had never been officially acknowledged, many of the people interviewed were prepared to make comments or give information. It was reported that Jeremy Hunt (Secretary of State for Health and Social Care 2012-2018), Sir Simon Stevens (Chief Executive Officer of NHS England) and Dame Sally Davies (Chief Medical Officer for England 2010-2019) were among the key players. The modelling for the exercise was carried out by the same team from Imperial College, London that has been tracking the progress of Covid-19 since it arrived in the UK. What precisely caused Exercise Cygnus to be undertaken was not made clear, but it seems likely that note had been taken of the two epidemics that had affected Asia earlier during the present century and that it had been concluded that it was only a matter of time before another Asian epidemic reached Europe and other parts of the world.

The exercise was apparently carried out over three days in October 2016, and the results were alarming to say the least. Severe shortages of vital equipment, particularly ventilators and intensive care beds, were highlighted. Personal Protective Equipment (PPE) for doctors, nurses and other health workers was in very short supply, and much of what was available was of poor quality and unsuitable for a pandemic. There was, it was revealed, a very real danger that in certain circumstances the NHS could be overwhelmed. In a worst-case scenario, the report added, 'medics would need to adopt a "battlefield" mentality, and prioritise patients according to their survival chances'! There were also significant gaps in what was referred to as the NHS's 'surge capacity' (presumably the NHS's ability to respond adequately to a sudden huge influx of infected people).

The timing of the exercise and of the report on its findings was somewhat unfortunate, as it occurred and was reported on, about four months after the June 2016 referendum, i.e., in the early days of the Theresa May government. The minds of the Prime Minister and of other senior ministers would have been focused strongly on the oncoming Brexit negotiations, and it might already have become obvious that Brexit was going to be extremely expensive. Therefore, although a senior government source was said to have stated that the results of Exercise Cygnus were not put in the public domain because they would terrify people, preoccupation with Brexit and an unwillingness to take on additional costs at that juncture may also have been factors. Whatever the true reasons might have been, the government clearly decided to kick the report into the long grass. To what extent the NHS was able to develop contingency planning from Exercise Cygnus is unclear, but in the absence of adequate NHS funding (a situation that continued for most of the following three years) there seems little that they could have done to address the shortages that Cygnus had revealed.

In the event, when Covid-19 arrived in the UK in early 2020, the NHS staff had no choice but to deal with the situation with the resources that were available, and the response that they made, and are continuing to make, has never been less than magnificent. Their work, particularly during the first year of the pandemic, often involved dealing with seriously ill victims of the virus with inadequate, or even non-existent, PPE and many of them paid a heavy price for their gallantry. It was their sacrifices, and the deaths of many people around the UK, that persuaded me to write this chapter. Many of the deaths of elderly people have occurred in care homes; casualties that were frequently preceded by the introduction into the care home of a person who had been treated for Covid-19 in hospital. With a severe shortage of intensive care beds, particularly during the early months of the pandemic, hospitals had no choice at times but to discharge partially recovered patients back into a care home within the local community. In such instances, the elderly residents residing in these care homes were little more than sitting ducks. A substantial number of care home employees also became ill, as, particularly in the early stages of the pandemic, they often lacked elementary PPE such as facemasks. Care homes in many cases have been neglected and underfunded in the UK for a long time, and their employees have not been given the recognition and support that they deserve.

What precisely might have been undertaken if there had been no Brexit and the NHS had been properly funded and staffed between 2016 and 2020? I believe that Exercise Cygnus, in the absence of Brexit, might well have been taken seriously, and that its main recommendations would probably have been accepted and acted upon. A thorough review of vital equipment and PPE could then have been made, and, where necessary and with the aid of appropriate sections of British industry, new improved designs of equipment could then have been developed and potential UK supply chains established. Similarly, with the involvement of appropriate organisations and, possibly, the armed forces, plans for emergency hospital buildings and additional intensive care beds could have been formulated. If the necessary foresight had been available, plans could also have been made to make emergency supplies of PPE and other vital equipment available to care homes. Although not an official part of the healthcare system, they too, particularly in emergency situations, have a vital role to play. The costs that would have been involved in taking all of these actions, although appreciable, would have been negligible compared with the amounts that had to be expended after Covid-19 struck. The UK was then having to compete with a host of other countries that were trying to obtain similar equipment, and, inevitably in this kind of situation, a great deal of money was wasted on sub-standard items. Regretfully, in the free-for-all for anti-pandemic equipment that ensued, it was reported that certain wealthy people were capitalising on the situation by buying up large quantities of items and re-selling them at a much higher price to the NHS.

When trying to assess how well or otherwise the UK has confronted

Covid-19, it was obviously advisable for me to concentrate on obtaining reliable statistical evidence from reputable sources. With this in mind, I contacted the Office for National Statistics, and they, using Eurostat information, provided me with much useful statistical information. It seemed that the most reliable information available that I could use when comparing the UK's performance with the performances of EU countries was the rcASMR (percentage) (relative cumulative age-standardised mortality rate percentage) data, or to put it more simply, the excess mortality rates. Unfortunately, the data that I received was only able to cover the period from January 2020 until June 2021, and is, therefore, over a year old. However, If I am able to obtain updated statistics before I finish this book, I will provide the latest figures. Nevertheless, these official figures make it clear that of the twenty-seven EU countries, only seven former Iron Curtain countries and Italy have had higher death rates from Covid-19 than the UK. Most northern European countries in the EU, particularly the Scandinavian countries, have had considerably lower death rates than the UK. The statistics that I have quoted above are backed up by the worldometer 'Deaths from Covid-19 per 1 million of population' figures (worldometer statistics are produced in the USA) for European countries which, although their reliability has been questioned, paint a similar picture.

What therefore is the cause of the UK's relatively poor performance against Covid-19, compared, for example, with Scandinavia, Germany, the Netherlands and Switzerland? We had a speedy roll-out of vaccines in this country, which undoubtedly saved the lives of many elderly people and for which Boris Johnson and his advisers deserve credit. There are probably a number of factors involved, e.g., the population densities in some parts of the UK, particularly in parts of England, may well be one. I personally have no doubt, however, that lack of preparation for a pandemic was a major factor. Even if we give the Brexiteer government of late 2016 the benefit of the doubt and accept that the costs of implementing the recommendations of Exercise Cygnus were probably not a major factor in their rejection of the exercise, it is still likely that preoccupation with Brexit was a factor. As far as the roll-out of vaccines in the EU is concerned, I believe that this would have started much earlier if the UK had still been a member. When important decisions needed to be made quickly in the EU, the UK's representatives, both politicians and officials, had acquired a reputation for getting things done, and I can see no reason why they would not have risen to the occasion in the case of the pandemic. Once the EU got started on its own roll-out of vaccines, several EU countries caught up with the UK quite rapidly and some were able to offer vaccines to younger age groups at an earlier date than the UK could achieve.

We are all aware of the heavy loss of life and the serious disruptions to normal activities that Covid-19 has caused in the UK, to say nothing of its huge strain on our country's resources, but what effect, if any, has it had upon Brexit? This might seem a strange thing to say about an infection that caused Prime Minister Boris Johnson to become seriously ill, but I believe that it has had at least two major benefits for Brexit. Boris Johnson was able to finalise his trade deal with the EU at a time when the UK was, understandably, pre-occupied with Covid-19. Without the pandemic, even allowing for the leader of the opposition's reluctance to criticise Brexit, the finer details of his trade deal would have been subjected to far greater scrutiny by both the media and by opposing politicians in Parliament. The BBC, especially, would have been obliged to study the deal more diligently, and it is possible that at least some of its deficiencies might have been exposed. The pandemic has also provided Brexit with a very useful scapegoat, which can take the greater part of the blame for the UK's heavy losses of revenue since Brexit. Covid-19 has indeed caused heavy losses, but so has Brexit; at least £360 billion so far. Whilst the former is frequently being blamed in the media, there is a conspiracy of silence about the latter. It could be said therefore that Covid-19 has unintentionally provided Brexit with a colossal smokescreen behind which Brexiteer politicians have been able to hide undisturbed. We can only hope that the effects of Covid-19 and of the war in the Ukraine lessen in the near future, and that this will enable the UK to give Brexit the critical scrutiny that it deserves.

Chapter 11

The Way Ahead

With so many crises affecting the UK at the present time, i.e., Covid-19, the Ukraine, climate change, inflation, heavy financial debts and spiralling energy prices, it is easier to propose an eventual destination for the UK than it is put forward a sensible route. The rapid rises in energy prices, in particular, are currently causing alarm to large sections of our population across the UK. EU countries, far from operating in an economic straitjacket as some Brexiteers would have us believe, have developed widely diverse methods of meeting their energy requirements. When we look at the two EU heavyweights, Germany and France, we see totally different ways of obtaining energy. Germany is heavily dependent on supplies of natural gas which until very recently have primarily been supplied by Russia. Their government, in the aftermath of Russia's invasion of the Ukraine, is now heavily engaged in attempting to obtain their much-needed gas supplies from other sources. France on the other hand has developed nuclear and renewable energy to meet much of its requirements, and its government has felt able to place price caps on both electricity and gas which will limit overall price increases, over a period which extends to beyond next winter, to about five per cent; a vastly superior energy situation for consumers to the one that the UK is now experiencing.

In the opening chapter of this book, I made it clear that I have always believed that the UK made a serious error in 1956 when it failed to opt for founder membership of the EEC. I also mentioned in that chapter that it seemed that the advantages that would accrue from founder membership would be considerable, but did not give further details of what I considered the advantages to be. This I will now remedy, as, unlike the Brexiteer politicians, I would not wish to get into the habit of making assertions without providing real evidence to support them. First, it needs to be realised that everything would have started from scratch; there were no agricultural or fisheries policies in existence and these would have been determined by the founder members. If the UK had opted to become a founder member, I think it likely that there would have been nine founder members rather than the original six. It seems certain that the Republic of Ireland would have joined at the same time, and that Denmark might also have taken part. Each and every founder member would have entered into the discussions and, although sensible compromises would have been necessary, it is likely from the UK's standpoint that a far more acceptable fisheries policy would have emerged. Similarly, it would probably have been possible to agree an agricultural policy which was better suited to UK farming, and which provided better access to the UK and other EEC markets for our traditional food sources, the old Commonwealth countries of Canada, Australia and New Zealand. It would not have been in the best interests of these countries to align themselves too closely to the EEC as they clearly needed to develop trade links within their own hemispheres, but it would have made the trading transitions easier for them and it might have been possible for them to devote a segment of their economies to the EEC. Another advantage that would have benefited the UK is the fact that our country would have been closely involved in the EEC's development from the outset. In the formation of what would eventually become the European Union, the UK would have been able to play a constructive role in the establishment of the EU's many institutions, and could have helped to ensure that democratic principles were maintained to the greatest possible degree. Although it would not be sensible to dwell too long on what might have been, I believe that it is useful to look at past mistakes and to use them to inform better decisions in the future.

The last ten years have been tumultuous ones for UK politics. The arrival of an enticing but dangerous fantasy that was supported by a majority of voters, the presence of sub-standard national leaders in both the Government and main opposition parties and the additional economic upheavals caused by Covid-19 and the Ukraine situation, have combined to create huge international debts and rampant inflation and have plunged the UK into crisis mode. By any reasonable and objective assessment, Brexit has been a total failure. The UK's current (19 August 2022) inflation rate of 10.1 per cent is appreciably higher than that of the other G7 countries, which are now standing at USA and Germany 8.5 per cent, Italy 8.4 per cent, Canada 7.6 per cent, France 6.8 per cent and Japan 2.4 per cent. In addition to energy prices, an increase in food prices is being given as one of the causes of the higher inflation rate, but that, of course, begs the question, 'Why have food prices risen more sharply in the UK than in other comparable European countries?'. One, if not the main, reason must surely be that almost twenty months since Brexit came into effect, food supply-chain problems are still playing a part. The massive losses of GDP revenue caused by Brexit (at least £370 billion so far) are still not being commented on in the media or by leading opposition politicians, and most of the British public are, in consequence, in blissful ignorance about them.

What therefore should be the way ahead for the UK? I have been looking carefully at the various options that might be available. The current leader of the main opposition party, Sir Keir Starmer, appears to favour trying to make the best of Boris Johnson's trade agreement with the EU. The possibilities however of being able to do this without making drastic changes to the structure of Boris Johnson's FTA seem to me to be extremely remote. I accept that, in a more friendly and less combative atmosphere, it might be possible to negotiate some minor improvements, but any idea that we might be able to recover an appreciable number of the benefits that we enjoyed as an EU member is (if I might borrow a phrase from Sir John Major's article at Note 2) blithe optimism on a Panglossian scale. If we embarked upon a Norway type solution, this would involve our re-entering the EU single market and our acceptance of freedom of movement of EU nationals into and out of the UK. Moreover, we would have no voice in any of the EU's institutions, and no ability to influence its policies. Another possibility is that we could carry on in the way that we have been doing for the last twenty months. I have no doubt that we could survive, albeit with a much poorer trading economy and a greatly reduced presence in the world. However, do we wish our country to settle for second or third best? I, personally, have no doubt that, although the journey might be long and difficult, attempting to rejoin the EU would be by far the best course of action for the UK.

There are, however, a number of difficulties that would need to be overcome before that could happen. There is, first of all, an urgent need to introduce a more democratic system of electing our governments; one that represents the views and opinions of a majority of the people that voted and avoids the tyrannies by a minority that are inherent in the present voting system. By any objective assessment, it is abundantly clear that the first-past-the-post (FTP) system, which has always been used for UK parliamentary elections, is no longer fit for purpose. Although this has been evident for many years, it was highlighted by the General Election of

12 December 2019, when the present Brexiteer Conservative government was enabled by FPTP to carry out an action that was clearly opposed by a substantial majority of the voters who had taken part in that election, i.e., to take the UK out of the EU. Opponents of proportional representation (PR), who are naturally keen to preserve their party's dominance, have put forward a large number of myths about PR, all of which can easily be debunked by the realities. It would be possible to write reams on this subject, but a single example will suffice. It is sometimes said that PR gives extremist parties greater opportunities to acquire representation in parliament. In fact, a sensible threshold of voters, e.g., five per cent, that must be obtained before representation can be gained, is usually enough to keep undesirable parties at bay. In cases when an extremist party has managed to get into its country's parliament, it has, under PR, never been able to gain political control. Only under FPTP has it been possible for an extremist party to gain control of a parliament, and we have a good example of this with our present Brexiteer Conservative government. Under Boris Johnson, they have managed to remove from parliament or exclude from office most of the moderate and more decent Conservative politicians, and have begun to infiltrate their supporters into important positions in the media, particularly in the news and current affairs sectors. They have also made unwelcome attempts to interfere with the workings of the judiciary, and to obtain a judiciary that is more compliant and ready to follow their wishes.

    At the present time, far more democracies around the world are using a form of PR than are using FPTP systems, and countries such as the UK and the USA that are still using FPTP for general elections are very much in the minority. Among the PR systems that would benefit the UK today, the additional member system (AMS) (also known as the mixed member proportional representation) and the single transferable vote (STV) would appear to be the frontrunners for adoption. I personally lean towards AMS, which is currently in use in Germany, New Zealand and the Scottish and Welsh parliaments, but either AMS or STV would make our general elections far more democratic and would be a vast improvement over our present FPTP system. There is an urgent need for Labour, the UK's main opposition party at the present time, to give wholehearted support to the introduction of PR, and, as I write, there are encouraging signs that this might be about to happen. If the Labour Party does agree to throw its weight behind a change in our voting system from FPTP to PR, this could, in due course, usher in a golden age for the UK. However, before this can happen, Labour must first win a general election under FPTP, and, in order to do this and establish a good working majority in parliament, total co-operation between Labour and other PR-supporting parties, the SNP, the Liberal Democrats and the Greens, on the lines that I suggested in Chapter 6, will be essential. As far as re-admission to the EU is concerned, I believe that the introduction of PR in UK elections would be an important pre-requisite to any application. I doubt that the EU would regard re-entry favourably if they thought that a future FPTP government might be elected that could institute withdrawal procedures once again.

Another possible stumbling block, which might prevent the UK from introducing a more democratic system for UK general elections and, thereafter, exploring the possibilities of rejoining the EU, may lie in the form of Sir Keir Starmer. To say that I have been disappointed so far in his leadership of the Labour Party would, I am truly sorry to say, be a huge understatement. In every general election that I can remember the Conservative Party has always made references to its alleged economic competence, and to the Labour Party's alleged failure to cost properly its projects. At the present time, we have a situation where successive Conservative governments have, during the last six and a quarter years, squandered truly enormous sums of money on a pipe-dream, and yet the

Labour leader and the main areas of the British media deem it appropriate to keep quiet about it. If a Labour government had, over a similar period of time, been responsible for the loss of just one quarter of the amounts thrown away on Brexit, critical references to the matter would never end. It would seem, however, that Brexit, which is still causing the UK to lose huge amounts of money annually, has now acquired sacred cow status and must not be mentioned. Let me make it clear that I would not have expected either Keir Starmer or the media to keep banging on about Brexit in the middle of a pandemic. It was only right, in this situation, that the latter should have held centre stage. The British public should, however, have been made aware of the dire effects of Brexit on the UK economy at an appropriate time.

As I write, Liz Truss has just been elected to lead the Conservative Party, and for the sake of our country I wish her the best of luck in the difficult task that she will be undertaking. In her short victory speech to the party faithful, she expressed the view that she will be able to win the 2024 General Election for them. I hope that she is wrong about that because, in the light of the damage that her party has inflicted upon the UK, I believe that the Conservative Party is in need of a full and genuine renaissance before it will be fit to lead our country again. She is, however, an energetic politician, who will get to grips with our country's problems quickly, and I expect to hear her introduce energy price caps within the next few days. What, unfortunately, is missing from her administration is any recognition of the fact that in 'getting Brexit done' the Boris Johnson government has made it far more difficult for the UK to ride out economic storms. The firm and reliable economic base that we once enjoyed has now been discarded, together with much of our national prestige and recognition as a country that keeps its word.

Whether it is prepared to recognise it or not, much of the responsibility for ensuring that the UK enters a new, progressive phase within the next few years now rests with the Labour Party and its leader, Sir Keir Starmer. There is an urgent need for the Labour Party to develop and maintain good relations with the other opposition parties and, in certain areas, to develop a common strategy. Previous experiences suggest that this will not be easy, but if, at the next general election, the Conservative Party's media advantages are to be overcome, full co-operation between the opposition parties will be essential. Keir Starmer has talked recently about the importance of looking forwards and not backwards, but he, and the other opposition parties, needs to understand that the UK has wandered into a cul-de-sac from which it will need to be extracted before genuine progress can be made. I was very disappointed when he, in effect, aligned his party with the Brexiteer government and directed that his MPs vote for Boris Johnson's trade agreement with the EU. There were manifest deficiencies in the FTA, and, at the very least, he should, I thought, have instructed his MPs to abstain when the vote was held. He was, I believe, concerned about the possibility of triggering a no-deal Brexit if his party voted against the FTA, but I do not see how abstention would have incurred that risk. His refusal, later, to draw attention to the huge financial losses that had been, and were still being, caused by Brexit, also appeared to me to be a very peculiar strategy. I believe that Labour are, at September 2022, slightly ahead in the opinion polls, but, in opposition over the last few years to the most financially reckless and incompetent government that I have known in my lifetime, they should by now be so far ahead as to be almost out of sight. I can only hope that Keir Starmer's strategy does, in due course, prove successful, and that, after winning the next general election, he follows a course of action that will truly be to the benefit of our great country.

I should now like to speak directly to the people who voted in the 2016 referendum. Addressing first the people who voted for Leave, I should like to say that, although I hope to have given most people food for thought, I do not expect a large proportion of leave voters to change their minds.

I recognise that many people have deeply ingrained views on this matter, and are probably impervious to the arguments that I have presented. However, I have been encouraged by the number of people who have posted messages on the RemainerNow site on Twitter. This has indicated to me that a substantial number of Leave voters are prepared to change their minds, and I would like, as far as possible, to encourage this action and gain their support. To any Leave voters who may be wavering or undecided, I should like them to ponder one fact. Of all the major countries in the world just one wanted the UK to leave the EU; the others advised the UK to remain in the EU. The one that wanted the UK to leave was, of course, Vladimir Putin's Russia, and the reason he wanted this was quite easy to understand. He knew that leaving the EU would weaken the UK, and that the EU itself would be weakened by the UK's absence. Regardless of the way people voted, I believe that they were all given a task that should not have been imposed upon the general public. Matters of great complexity and multiple ramifications should be the province of the people whom we elect to govern the UK. Harold Wilson, in my opinion, set a very bad precedent in 1975 when he organised our first referendum; a referendum that was, of course, concerned with the same subject, i.e., whether we should remain in or leave the EU. As far as Remain voters are concerned, you should know that, regardless of the reasons that prompted you to vote remain, you made the right call. Although the odds may now appear to be stacked against you, be prepared to carry on the fight to re-join the EU and do not despair. You now need to show as much tenacity and strength of purpose in a good cause as the leading Brexiteers, following their crushing defeat in the 1975 referendum, showed in a bad one.

By the end of next month (October 2022), I shall have reached ninety-five years of age, and, in the natural order of events, it seems unlikely that I will live long enough to see the UK restored to its rightful place as a great European nation within a great European confederation, the EU. However,

I do hope to be still around when the next general election takes place, and subsequently to see positive moves towards a more democratic and fairer UK. A new and fully functioning PR system for electing governments would be a useful first step in the right direction. Meanwhile, I hope that as many people as possible join the crusade that I envisage, and that it eventually arrives at a sensible outcome; the re-introduction of the UK into an invigorated and beneficial EU. At the present time in the UK there are many pro-EU organisations that are pursuing similar objectives, and it would be great if they could all get together to form one giant umbrella organisation. When one million people marched through London in support of staying in the EU, this was an astonishing indication of the strength of feeling about this matter that exists in the UK. Typically, I regret to say, the BBC endeavoured to play the event down as much as possible and insisted on giving equal publicity to Nigel Farage's pathetically small counter-march that occurred a short time afterwards.

Finally, and this really is my last word on Brexit (for the time being), I should like to give a short explanation of the impulses that prompted me to write this book. I had been extremely disappointed by the refusal of opposition politicians in parliament to enlighten the general public about the effects of Brexit and to give it the degree of criticism that it deserved, and eventually decided that, if they were not prepared to put their heads above the parapet, I would have to do it. In saying this, I in no way wish to belittle the many excellent and erudite books about Brexit that have already been published. Rather, I believed that I could present certain aspects about this contentious subject that had not previously been covered. I hope that I have succeeded in doing this, and that my country will eventually be able to pursue policies that lead to greater prosperity and better standards of living for all its people.

Albert Kemp

P.S. Since I completed this book about a month ago, there has been a great deal of political turmoil in the UK, and I have felt constrained to write a short postscript. I wrote earlier in Chapter 11 that recent Conservative administrations had been the most financially reckless and economically incompetent governments that I have known in my lifetime, but had not expected further proof of this to be provided so quickly. When, a few weeks ago, Liz Truss and her Chancellor, Kwasi Kwarteng, introduced a mini-budget which they hoped would stimulate growth in the economy, it instead created an unwelcome chain reaction which caused consternation in financial markets and uproar within her own Conservative Party. Liz Truss has, so far, managed to remain in power, but she has sacked her Chancellor, Kwasi Kwarteng, and replaced him with Jeremy Hunt. The PM was apparently aiming for a long-term GDP growth of two and a half percent, but does this not beg the question, 'What was wrong with the three per cent growth that the UK achieved in 2014 when still a member of the EU?'; a growth rate that was obtained without disturbing the markets and at a time when growth in most G7 and EU countries was depressed!

Endnotes

NOTE 1
Below are copies of emails that I sent to Paddy Ashdown and Gordon Brown on 11 June 2016 and 14 June 2016, respectively, in response to emails that I had received from their offices.

Paddy Ashdown

Memo in response to e-mail dated 10 June 2016 to Albert E Kemp

Thank you for your e-mail. I, too, am becoming increasingly concerned about the result of the referendum. In particular, I have been worried about the repeated failure of the Remain Forces to confront the Brexit politicians directly on the subject of immigration, as in my many conversations that I have had with individual members of the public this topic has usually been uppermost in their minds.

Before giving my views on Immigration, I would like to tell you something about myself. I am 88 years of age, have been retired for many years and have no business interests whatsoever. My sole concern is for the future welfare and prosperity of my Country. The varied jobs that I performed during my working life as a Civil Servant included an 11 year stint as an Immigration Officer (before we entered the EU). During this period, in addition to routine immigration work, I was involved in a number of political asylum cases, both as an interviewer and an interpreter.

It is my belief that if the Leave Campaign were to be successful in this referendum, immigration into the U.K. would actually increase rather than decrease. I think that there would be no change as far as EU citizens are concerned, but that the volume of refugees and economic migrants from outside the EU would increase dramatically.

First, with regard to EU citizens, I believe that the Leave Campaign's utterances are nothing more than a cynical ploy to obtain votes by deception. The clue to this is in the form of words that all the Brexit politicians have been using, which usually talk about 'the need for the UK to take back control of its own borders'. It was obvious to me that this repeated statement (clearly an agreed form of words) was both vague and misleading. It was misleading because we have never given up control of our own borders, and vague because it said nothing specific. After all, if they really intended to restrict EU migration to the UK they could easily have said, 'If our campaign is successful, we will restrict EU migration to the UK by re-imposing immigration controls on EU citizens'. When I thought a little about this, the reason for their choice of words seemed obvious to me; they had been chosen, not simply because they made a good sound-bite, but precisely because they were vague and misleading. The Leave Campaign wished to give the impression that they would restrict EU immigration into the UK without actually saying so.

The Brexit politicians are all, in varying degrees, fanatical in their dislike of the EU, but I do not believe that they are completely blind to the fact that if they do obtain a vote to leave the EU they would need to negotiate a favourable trade deal with the EU as soon as possible. By favourable, I mean a deal which mirrors the access which we currently enjoy. In doing this, they would have to make concessions to the EU which, undoubtedly, would include free movement of EU citizens into and out of the UK and the payment of a very large annual sum (probably as much as we presently pay plus the rebate); hence, their reluctance to single out EU citizens. In recent days, they have been talking about the introduction of an immigration points system on the Australian model, but this, too, has been in fairly vague terms. EU migration to the UK, unlike immigration from many other parts of the world, is not driven by civil war, famine, persecution or corruption. It is almost entirely job related, and when suitable jobs are in short supply the word will soon get back to their home countries and their numbers will reduce.

The position regarding refugees and economic migrants from outside the EU would, in the event of a Brexit success, be much more serious. There are unprecedented numbers of these unfortunate people around the world, particularly in parts of Africa and Asia, and many would welcome an opportunity to get to the UK, where they could claim asylum. Around a million and a half such people are said to have entered the EU via Italy and Greece during the last 15 to 18 months. The UK has been largely insulated from this huge influx, partly by the extraordinary generosity of some fellow EU countries but also because the EU has, effectively, been acting as a buffer zone. I have for some time been telling people that this zone will disappear if we leave the EU, and that immigrants arriving in Southern Europe would simply be fast-tracked through Europe to the UK. It seems obvious to me that, if we vote to leave, the French Authorities will lose no time in giving the required six-months notice to get rid of the UK Border Officials who are currently operating in their territory (the French public would insist upon it). We would then find refugees and others arriving on our doorstep in numbers that we simply would not be able to cope with. My views on these outcomes were confirmed recently when a very old school-friend of my wife's paid us a visit from France. She is an Englishwoman (now a widow) who married a Frenchman and has lived in France for most of her life Without any prompting from us, she told us that many French people were saying that, in the event of a British vote to leave the EU, they would ship any migrants that arrive in France straight through to the UK.

I am not indifferent to the plight of the Syrian refugees and the tragedy that has befallen their Country, and I hope that the UK will be able to assist them as much as possible. Nevertheless, the movement of refugees into the EU is becoming a huge problem, and one that needs to be solved at the EU level. It would be a tragedy if the UK were obliged to take unilateral action, e.g. withdrawing from the UN 1951 Convention, to overcome a situation that could well become critical if Brexit is successful.

I have jotted down these thoughts as they have occurred to me, and I hope that they are not too rambling and disjointed. I think that there is now an urgent need for a high-profile Remain politician to have a head to head tv debate on immigration with a senior Brexit man, e.g. Michael Gove, Ian Duncan-Smith or Boris Johnson. Time is now short, and doing nothing is not going to win the day.

I hope that the Remain Camp might be able to use some of the information that I have given. If anyone would like to contact me by telephone to discuss any of the points that I have raised, I am available on 01932 341839.

Albert E Kemp

Dear Gordon

Many thanks for your e-mail. I was pleased to see that you are now taking a leading role in the debate. As an 88 year old who spent 11 years of his life working as an Immigration Officer, I have been dismayed at the way in which media commentators and interviewers have accepted the Leave Campaign's mantra that leaving the EU would significantly reduce immigration into the UK. In my view our departure from the EU would be far more likely to *increase migration into the UK rather than decrease it. The Brexit stance on EU immigration is a complete sham, and nothing more than a cynical ploy to obtain votes by deception. They know perfectly well that in the event of a successful Leave vote a favourable Trade Agreement with the EU would be essential, and that freedom of movement by EU citizens into and out of the UK would be one of the main conditions that we would have to meet.*

As far as refugees and economic migrants from outside the EU are concerned, the numbers of such people arriving on our doorstep would increase dramatically. If the UK does vote to leave the EU, the French Authorities will lose no time in getting rid of the UK Border Control officials, who are operating in Northern France, as soon as possible. The way will then be open to fast-track non-EU people who arrive in Southern Europe straight through to the UK. A recent visitor to my home from France (an old school friend of my wife's) confirmed, without any prompting from us, that these actions are precisely what will occur.

I hope that you and the other Remain leaders are successful in your efforts to rebut the lies and deceits that are being practiced by the Leave camp.

Yours sincerely
Albert Kemp

On 13-Jun-16 8:40 PM, Gordon Brown, Stronger In Campaign wrote:

Dear Albert,
Voting to Remain is about a positive, stronger future. It is stronger for jobs, for rights at work and for maintaining a British voice on the world stage.
  But we shouldn't just be a member of the EU. We must be a leader.

By leading in Europe we can create more jobs in Britain, deliver higher living standards through energy price cuts, tackle tax havens, protect workers' rights and fight terrorism. If we're unhappy with the status quo, the best way to change it is to lead in Europe, not to leave it.

Today I spoke about why voters from Labour – and all political parties - have so much to gain from remaining.

Please share the video below, which I recorded recently in Coventry Cathedral, on Facebook or Twitter – or forward this email to your friends and family – so everyone knows we are better off IN Europe.

We don't want to be a 'fax democracy' like Norway or Switzerland. Outside Europe, they receive the decisions from Europe and they have to implement them. You have to be at the table, you have to be a negotiator – I know from my own experience that that is absolutely essential.

Together, let's campaign for a Britain we can be proud of: not isolated, not on the sidelines, but engaging in the world, out there leading with proposals, showing that we can change the world for the better.

Let's do it together.

Thank you,
Gordon Brown

NOTE 2

The article below was published in the Daily Telegraph during the 2016 Referendum campaign, and was written by Sir John Major. It has been reproduced verbatim in its entirety, and in its original format.

Comment by Sir John Major
This June, the UK will vote upon whether to leave or remain in the European

Union. This vote will be momentous. It will decide Britain's place in the world for generations to come.

There are many positive reasons for membership.

When we joined the EU, we were the 'sick man' of Europe. Today, as a result of our domestic reforms and membership of the European Single Market, we have the best performing economy in Europe.

Within the next 20 years – on present policies, and with continuing full access to the Single Market – the UK is likely to be the biggest economy in Europe.

And surely – in a global market drawing ever closer together – it is verging on the reckless for us to seek divorce from the world's pre-eminent trading bloc?

On issues such as the environment, climate change, internet costs and consumer protection, the UK can best progress – or sometimes only progress – in unity with our fellow Europeans.

In an uncertain world, the UK, as part of the EU, is better able to face up to the aggressive policies of hostile nations. We are safer, because the EU has brought together former enemies to face common perils. In the last thousand years of history, no previous generation has been so fortunate.

It would be sheer folly to put this all at risk
Beyond the positive advantages of membership, we have protection from many aspects of the EU that we dislike; we are not in the eurozone – because I kept us out of it over 20 years ago; we are not part of Schengen (and thus have control of our borders); and we have opted out of "ever closer union". We can veto any treaty that enhances EU powers.

We are the only nation within the EU which has managed to secure these concessions. It would surely be perverse to turn our back on these advantages, and replace them with serious risks that alarm our international friends and repel the inward investments that boost our jobs and living standards.

Suppose we left? What are the risks? They are many and real – and simply cannot be brushed aside with flippant slogans such as "Project Fear".

Consider this: as a Member State, the UK can (and does) influence European policies – often to our advantage, and sometimes simply to minimise damage to our own domestic interests. Outside, we would not be able to influence them at all. And yet, if – as a non-Member – we wish to retain access to the Single Market, we will be compelled to follow EU rules, over which we would have no influence at all. This is not only demeaning, it is a recipe for economic self-harm.

The "leave" campaign blandly assumes that once they have undermined – if not wrecked- the power of the EU by leaving it, they can simply renegotiate all the advantages of membership with pliant Europeans eager for our trade.

This is self-deception to the point of delusion. Their argument is that the EU needs the UK market more than we need theirs, on the basis that – overall – the EU exports more to the UK than we export to them. This is, at best, disingenuous.

More bluntly, it is fantasy

UK exports to Europe represent nearly 45 per cent of our total exports. On average – across the EU – the other 27 member states send only 7 per cent of their total exports to us.

In the game of who needs who the most, the answer is clear. Our European partners will not be the demandeur in any negotiations on the Single Market – we will be.

Moreover, if we left, it is blithe optimism on a Panglossian scale for the "leave" campaign to assume that our partners – having been rebuffed and deserted in an EU diminished by our departure – will be well disposed and eager to accede to our demands.

I fear the reverse will be true. Resentment will be deep. The broken relationship is more likely to be poisonous than harmonious. The UK will have chosen to leave and, by so doing, will have gravely weakened the whole of the EU. Our partners will not wish to reward us for that – indeed, they may well be more inclined to resist our demands to discourage other nations from leaving it.

In time, the EU will no doubt do a trade deal with us – but it will certainly not be a sweetheart deal; and negotiating it is likely to be harder and harsher than the optimists believe. And if we wish such a deal to include services (such as banking and insurance), or to prevent hidden non-tariff barriers – which we do, since both are crucial to our well-being – it may be a long time coming.

Of course – and "leave" campaigners please note – the price of any deal with significant access to the Single Market is that we will be forced to accept free movement of people, and pay into the EU budget. Without that, as Germany's finance minister has made clear, there will be no deal. These are realities that the "leave" campaign must face up to and address, so that the British people are able to reach their decision based on facts. Instead, they ignore – even obscure – the facts, to hide the weakness of their case.

"Give us our country back" is an emotional appeal that warms the heart of all those who love our country, as I do. But it is a meaningless sound bite. An illusion. A prelude to disappointment. And what country, exactly, will we "get back"? Will Scotland remain part of the UK? As a Unionist, I hope so – but no one should ignore the threat that if the UK-wide vote is to leave, Scotland may demand another referendum on independence. The UK out of the EU and Scotland out of the UK would be a truly awful outcome.

Let everyone be clear; no one can be certain of the scale of the fallout from leaving the EU. But there are many legitimate risks, and not even the most optimistic "leave" advocate can wave them away. We have been warned against exit – by America, China, Japan; are all these large investors in the UK to be ignored? Should we also ignore the G20? The Governor of the Bank of England? Our military leaders? Our leading scientists and academics? A majority of large and small businesses? Are they really all guilty of "interfering, "scaremongering", or being part of one enormous plot being orchestrated by No 10? Such a notion is absurd.

Would we remain such a pre-eminent ally of the United States if we no longer had influence in the EU? Close, yes – because of trade; important, yes – because of history; but outside the EU, part of our influence would wane.

In our absence, the US would need a powerful friend within the EU - and it could no longer be us.

Our departure would not only weaken the UK, but Europe, too. If the UK left, the EU would lose;

 # The fastest-growing economy in it;
 # One of only two nuclear powers;
 # The country with the longest and deepest foreign-policy reach.

As a result of a UK exit, the political influence of the EU would be diminished – especially when considered against the power of the US or China.

Without the UK, Europe – the cradle of modern civilisation – would fall to a lower significance. I cannot believe that any sensible Briton wishes to divide Europe, and thus divide the West; only our enemies could gain from that, as John McCain, the US senator, has made clear in recent days. No doubt the "leave" campaign will accuse him of "scaremongering" too.

The Referendum decision on June 23 is not a prelude to further negotiation. It will be final. Our nation can either decide to be true to our history – and remain outward-looking internationalists on the world stage – or shrink to lower prominence.

It will be a fateful choice; Great Britain or Little Britain
As our children and grandchildren look back at this pivotal moment in our history, I hope they can be proud that, in a world of uncertainties – of Daesh [Isil], of Syria, of Putin's Russia – our country did not turn its back on Europe and cripple its authority, but chose to remain in it, reform it, and

play our part in maximising British influence and European power for the common good.

NOTE 3

On a number of occasions in this book, I have given the monetary values of percentages of GDP (Gross Domestic Product). The information that enabled me to do this was furnished by, the then, Chancellor of the Exchequer, Rishi Sunak, when he stated whilst introducing his furlough scheme that the £330 billion that he intended to make available for the scheme was equivalent to 15% of GDP. From this, I was able to deduce that 1% of GDP would have a value of £22 billion, and from this information it was easy to calculate the values of percentages given as and when they were needed.

NOTE 4

The article below was published by the Guardian on 12 March 2019, and written by a former Prime Minister of Australia, Kevin Rudd. Apart from the opening sentence, which was incomplete in the transcript that I received, I have reproduced it verbatim and in its original form.

"***************************** *relationship with the European Union. This is the nuttiest of the many nutty arguments that have emerged from the Land of Hope and Glory set now masquerading as the authentic standard-bearers of British patriotism. It's utter bollocks.*

If Britain proceeds with giving effect to what future historians will legitimately describe as the longest suicide note in history by leaving the union, the cold, hard reality is that the mathematics simply don't stack up in terms of credible economic alternatives to Europe. Much as any Australian, Canadian and New Zealand governments of whichever persuasion would do whatever they could to frame new free-trade agreements with the UK, the bottom line is that 65 million of us do not come within a bull's roar of Britain's adjacent market of 450 million Europeans.

As for India, good luck! India's trade and commerce bureaucracy is the most mercantilist and outright protectionist in the world. They virtually single-handedly sank the Doha round in 2009. In the same year, as prime minister of Australia, I launched a free-trade negotiation with Delhi. But a decade later, those negotiations remain at a standstill. The Australian economy is only 50% the size of Britain's. A substantive India-UK FTA is the ultimate mirage constructed by the Brexiteers. It's as credible as the ad they plastered on the side of that big red bus about the £350m Britain was allegedly paying to Brussels each week. Not.

So as a former chair of the Commonwealth ministerial action group, it's my melancholy duty to report that the idea the old (or for that matter newer) Commonwealth could possibly substitute for Britain's current economic arrangements with Brussels is an illusion.

Then the Brexiteers turn to that other great economic chimera, the US, as final salvation. The irony is that the current wave of nationalism, isolationism and protectionism that they so ruthlessly exploited in the Brexit referendum has also been unleashed in the US. Donald Trump's America has little, if any, room in its political imagination for maintaining existing bilateral free trade agreements (see Nafta and Korea), let alone negotiating mutually advantageous new ones. Let's not forget the very first act of the Trump administration was to withdraw from the Trans-Pacific Partnership, despite the economic damage done to three of its closest allies – Australia, Canada and Japan. If No. 10 still thinks its "special relationship" with the White House will uniquely be capable of battering down the doors of a newly protectionist America, then good luck with that one too.

In Australia, we have our own Land of Hope and Glory set who have been cheering the Brexiteers on to victory, as chaps would cheer on the home *side at a good game of rugger on the playing fields of Eton. By and large, however, these Oz-Brexiteers have been confined to the right wing of the Australian conservatives and no longer represent the Australian political mainstream. They too, like the core of the British Brexiteers, are driven by a conservative political romanticism that we can all somehow go back to that ancient Arcadia of a white Anglo-Saxon world with "imperial preference", all consummated by the solemnity of a Lord's Test. Former prime minister Tony Abbott, for example, recently invoked the spirit of Wellington, Nelson and Drake in the pages of the Spectator in defence of the most ludicrous of all the Brexit possibilities – the no-deal, cold turkey outcome. Abbott's message: the old empire is just champing at the bit for Britain to cut itself loose from all those continentals in Brussels. That too is bollocks.*

For obvious cultural reasons, practically all Australians like Britain. They want Britain to do well. They are happy with the idea of allowing their kids to live and work in Britain, just as we welcome British kids in Australia. But with the best will in the world, we cannot turn the clock back to 1973 when Britain joined the EEC and told Australia to go carve out its economic future elsewhere. So we did – but following Britain's example in Europe, we set about integrating our economy with our neighbours in the Asia-Pacific region.

Beyond Britain's economic self-interest, there is a further reason why the UK needs to remain in the EU. It's about the future of the very idea of the west itself, of western values and their wider contribution to the future of the international order. For centuries, Europe and the US have been the joint custodians of the western tradition – Judeo-Christianity, the Enlightenment and the political, economic and social freedoms of the current century. These in turn have helped shape many of the international norms underpinning the current order.

However, the US's future commitment to the very idea of the west, and western values in foreign policy terms, is now the subject of fundamental debate within the US body politic. It may prove to be a temporary, Trumpian aberration. But we would be foolish not to identify a new isolationism emerging.

If the American pillar is looking a little shaky, Europe is looking even shakier. The strength of the political emergence of the far right across Europe's four largest economies – Germany, France, Italy and Spain – is frightening. The European political centre is being hollowed out. All at a time when Europe's economy is once again weakening. And that's before you add the final blow to the solar-plexus in the form of Brexit. The bottom line is that a European Union without Britain will be a weaker international actor than it has been, particularly if the European centre of political gravity increasingly moves in a more populist direction. Without a strong Europe, the continuing idea of "the west" begins to look very weak indeed. And authoritarians around the world would like nothing more than a fully disembowelled west, no longer confident of what it actually stands for any more.

So my appeal to Brits, both Conservative and Labour, is to use this critical fortnight to start turning all this around. For Britain's economic self-interest, as well as the wider political interests of the western community of nations, Britain should remain in the EU. Labour and the Conservative remainers should unite to defer the exit date beyond 29 March 2019. They should then support legislation for a second referendum – offering the British people a clear, informed choice between two tangible, concrete proposals: either voting for Theresa May's deal, or for Britain to remain in the Union. That's when I believe Briton's native common sense, as well as their wider sense of international responsibility, would ultimately prevail."

SYNOPSIS

The author, by providing information about knowledge that he gained during a visit to Strasbourg University in September 1956, first draws attention to the rarely acknowledged but serious error that the United Kingdom made in 1956 when it failed to opt for founder membership of the European Economic Community. He then, in order to let the public have some information about himself, gives personal details about his immediate family, the area of east London where he was born and grew up and his own early life. From this point, the emphasis is entirely upon Brexit, about which he has many forthright and trenchant views, e.g., the way in which the 2016 referendum could and should have been avoided, the latter's coverage on tv and radio which left much to be desired and the Brexiteer fantasies that are largely responsible for the economic and structural damage that is currently being caused to the United Kingdom. The main events concerning Brexit, and many of the personalities involved, are commented upon, and a way out of the morass is advocated in the final chapter.